You Are Hired! Job Interview Preparation

Stand Out From the Crowd, Know Exactly What to Answer, Show Them What You're Worth and Get Your Dream Job + Top Most Common Questions & Answers

Job Interview Preparation

Table of Contents

Introduction 5
Chapter 1—Score the Interview 9
   How to Land More Job Interviews Immediately. 9
   Tips for Building a Resume that Can Get You Hired. 13
   Cover Letters: Why You Need One and How to Make Yours Irresistible. 16
Chapter 2—Dress to Conquer 21
   What to Wear if You're a Man. 21
   What to Wear if You're a Woman. 24
   Six Things You Should Not Wear to an Interview. 27
   The Truth About Tattoos and Piercings. 29
Chapter 3—Prepare Like a Boss 34
   How to Overcome Anxiety and Nervousness. 34
   Nine Things You Need to Research for Your Interview. 39
   Other Vital Ways to Prepare for Your Job Interview 44
Chapter 4—Questions and Answers 49
   12 Common Interview Questions and How to Ace Them. 49
   Navigating Difficult Questions Like a Champion. 56
Chapter 5—Make a Great First Impression 62
   Eight Things You Must Do to Make a Killer First Impression. ... 62
   How to Instantly Stand Out Among Other Candidates. 67
   Confident Body Language that Puts You Ahead of the Game. 70

Chapter 6—Pass with Flying Colors 73
   11 Things Your Prospective Employer Wants to Hear 73
   Eight Things You Won't Want to Say in a Job Interview. 75
   10 Soft Skills and How to Demonstrate Them. 76

Chapter 7—Finishing Touches 82
   11 Great Questions to Ask the Hiring Manager. 82
   An Essential Guide to Salary Negotiations 86
   What to Do When You Get a Question that Throws You Off-Guard. 89
   Is It OK to Lie?; When Is It OK to Lie in an Interview? 90

Chapter 8—The Future is Waiting 94
   What to do after the job interview. 94
   You Got the Job! Now what? 96
   How to Transform a Rejection into Something Positive. 99

Conclusion 104

Job Interview Preparation

Introduction

For most of us, we had to learn to crawl before we could learn to walk. The same goes with finding the job of your dreams. Before you can get the job you've always wanted, you'll have to get an interview for the job. And then you'll have to ace that interview, passing it with flying colors and positioning yourself above other candidates for the same job. Many great candidates have lost job opportunities because they either were not able to get interviews or they came up empty in the interviews they had. Maybe they didn't have a resume that stood out above other candidates. Maybe their cover letter was lacking. Maybe they didn't dress appropriately for the interview. Maybe they didn't prepare properly. Maybe they got stumped by a question in the interview or maybe they said something wrong. Maybe, maybe, maybe… In getting and then acing interviews, it's extremely important that you have a plan and a process which gives you the best chance possible to get the job you're looking for.

In this book, I'm going to give you the tools and techniques you'll need to score interviews for the jobs you're interested in. I'm also going to tell you the things you'll need to do in the interview itself, including how to prepare for questions, how to dress, how to navigate difficult questions, what questions to ask prospective employers, how to broach and negotiate salary, and what to do in following up after the interview. All in all, I'll tell you how to position yourself above other candidates who are applying for the same job.

My name is David Allen. I am a how-to-get-a-job expert. I have years of experience as a human resources director for multiple companies in different industries. I've also worked as a recruiter, recruiting people to fill various corporate job openings. And finally, I also work as a career counselor, helping people find optimum career paths or jobs that will enable them to live happy, healthy, and successful lives. Over the years, I've noted that so many people are unable to get the jobs they want, simply because they don't know how to get interviews, how to prepare for interviews, or how to perform in the actual interview itself. Many of my clients who have had success based on the knowledge I've provided, have encouraged me to detail my knowledge in the form of a book. With this book, I've now done that, in the hopes that I'll be able to help a lot more people in their efforts to get the jobs they want.

If you can implement some of the tips and techniques I'm providing in this book, you'll enhance your chances of getting interviews for the jobs you're interested in and, subsequently, landing the jobs you really want. As a career counselor, I've worked with clients who had been trying for years to get the interviews or the jobs they were interested in. These clients came to me because they were not successful in their efforts and they wanted to know how they could improve their chances of securing the jobs they were looking for. In following some of the simple recommendations and steps I provided, these clients immediately found that they were having more success in getting interviews and in the results of those interviews. Many of these clients were unaware of what they were doing wrong, the things that made them unsuccessful in their efforts. With some simple tweaking, I was able to help these clients get the jobs they wanted.

Whether these clients were looking to find a job in which they made more money, find a job which utilized their talents more adequately, or find a job which had a better work environment, I was able to point them in the right direction and work with them in developing a plan or a process which enabled them to be successful in their pursuit of the job they wanted. Through the years, I've received emails, phone calls, and handwritten notes thanking me for my help in this process. Some of my clients have even told me that the information and advice I provided was life-altering. I sincerely hope that I can make the same impact on your job search and possibly even your career. I'd be delighted to receive a note from you someday soon telling me that in this book I provided you with tips and techniques you used to land the job of your dreams.

If you'll read this short book and follow the tips and techniques I've provided, I'll assure you that you'll increase your chances to get job interviews and also increase the chances of getting the job itself. Before you can land the job you really want, you'll need to get the interview. Baby steps…you'll have to learn to crawl before you can learn to walk. And then once you get the interview, there are some surefire ways to ensure that you can be your best self in acing that interview. Getting a job is an activity that requires a plan and a process. Throughout this book, I will encourage you to develop a solid plan and then to focus more on the process of being your best self in trying to get the job you want instead of focusing on the results of your efforts. If you can develop a plan based on my recommendations and then work that plan, I'll assure you that you will enhance your chances of getting the job you really want.

I've read before that self-help or how-to books of this nature generally illicit two different types of calls to action: Some readers will tuck the knowledge that is offered into the remote regions of their memory banks, saying that they'll implement those ideas at a later date, whenever they get around to it. For the most part, these people are generally unsuccessful in their efforts, as "life happens"/time passes and they never get around to implementing the plan they said they would someday implement. The other type of reader is the type who will take the information gained and implement it immediately. I only hope that you are this type of reader, as these are the people who are much more likely to be successful in their efforts. If you'll implement immediately the tips in this book which are appropriate to you, you'll be much more likely to be successful in landing interviews and jobs. No, I can't guarantee that you'll get the job you're interested in, but I will guarantee that you'll have a much better chance to do so. Again, the key will be to focus on the process of getting interviews and jobs as compared to the results.

The tips and techniques in this book have been proven to be successful. If you will take the time to read this short book and then implement a plan based on the information the book provides, you'll increase your chances to get the interviews and the jobs you really want. Each chapter of this book has specific tips and techniques which can help you be successful in your job-hunting efforts. So, that being said, "Let's get after it"!

Chapter 1—Score the Interview

Looking for a job can be a daunting task. It can be tedious, stressful, and disappointing. But, by breaking this down into individual tasks, you can make substantial progress in just a short amount of time. As mentioned before, you won't be able to get a job unless you get an interview first. With this in mind, this chapter outlines the best ways to ensure that you get interviews.

How to Land More Job Interviews Immediately.

Whenever you try to secure an interview with a prospective employer, it's extremely important for you to keep in mind that in, in almost all instances, you'll be one of multiple people applying for that job. With this in mind, you're going to have to make sure that you stand out from other applicants.

First of all, you should determine exactly what kind of position you want to apply for and also, if possible, what kind of company you would like to work for. As an example, if you have a marketing background and you are interested in a marketing job, I would suggest that you narrow your search within those parameters. A client of mine, who was looking to make a job change, had a background in restaurant marketing for two different franchised restaurant chains. He enjoyed different aspects of both these jobs, however he had grown stagnant with the restaurant company he was working for. So, in realizing that he enjoyed working in the restaurant and hospitality industry and also realizing that companies within the restaurant industry would value his experience, my client opted to look for a job within the restaurant industry. To narrow the field even further, he realized that his experience of working for a franchised company would be particularly attractive to another franchised restaurant company.

So, he targeted restaurant companies in his job search and narrowed the field even more by selecting some franchised restaurant companies in his search. He was fully aware of the things he could bring to the table for a restaurant company or a franchised company that other applicants might not be able to offer. So, instead of applying to be a marketing person in a tech company or an architectural company in which he had no experience (and not much interest), my client decided to target franchised restaurant groups. Also, it should be noted that he targeted a few companies which consisted mostly of company-owned restaurants and a few companies in other franchised industries, including a franchised health club chain and a franchised print shop chain. In other words, my client took a personal inventory of his experience and his likes and then used that information to determine the types of companies to which he wanted to submit applications.

Once he did that, he adjusted his resume to fit that particular industry or those particular companies. For instance, with the franchised health club chains, he mentioned early in his resume that he had considerable experience in working with franchisees from all different areas of the country. He was aware that the franchised health club chain, which had started in one area of the company, was now expanding to other areas of the country and he he realized that this experience of working with franchisees in different areas of the country would likely be particularly valuable to the company he was interested in working for. Although I'll give you additional tips on how to develop a resume that stands out later in this chapter, I'll tell you now that it will be very important for you to continue to tweak and adjust your resume based on the companies you are sending it to. No, you can't just develop one resume, make 100 copies of that resume, and then send it out for every

Job Interview Preparation

job you're interested in. If you want to be successful in getting interviews, you'll need to continue to fine tune your resume for each job you're applying for.

Another way to ensure that you'll land more interviews will be to prepare and update your personal marketing materials before you even begin sending out resumes. Do you have business cards that you can hand out at networking events or any time you meet someone who could be a possible job source for you? Do you have a LinkedIn profile? (If not, you should have one.) If you have a LinkedIn profile, have you updated that profile? Are you present on social media platforms such as Facebook, Instagram, and Twitter? If so, do those sites convey you as a person who would be an asset to a company that is hiring? Is there any negative information on those sites that might impact your chances of landing a job? If so, can that information be deleted? Or, if it can't be deleted, is it something that can be addressed or justified if a prospective employer asks you about it in an interview? Do you have your own personal web page or a blog site? If not, are these things that might help you secure a new job? If you have a personal web site or blog site, make sure those sites reflect a positive image to a prospective employer.

In trying to determine which companies might be hiring, it's important to note that an extraordinary number of job openings are not advertised. I've seen research which shows that over 90% of all jobs are not advertised. Although this seems a bit high to me, the importance of the thought should not be lost...most job openings are not posted. With this in mind, I'll tell you that even though it is certainly important for you to search job boards when looking for jobs, you should never stop there. Companies often don't post jobs on job boards because they don't want to be swamped with resumes, many from candidates who are not qualified. Other companies prefer to solicit their own candidates through internal postings or by searching through resumes on LinkedIn or other job platforms and then inviting qualified candidates to interview. Other companies will hire recruiters, often referred to as headhunters, to bring candidates to them.

And finally, in your efforts to find out about job openings and secure interviews, I strongly encourage you to network. Network, network, network. Even if you don't participate regularly with any organized networking groups or professional organizations, I encourage you to have a "networking mindset", which means that you are consistently telling people about the positions you are looking for. I always like to tell the following story, which comes from a client of mine. She was looking for an accounting job in a specific major retail store chain. Her research had told her that this company was a great company to work for, however she had no contacts there and no way to get her foot in the door for an interview. She made a habit of telling most of the people she knew that she was interested in getting an interview with this particular company she had targeted. Eventually, when she was at her hair salon, she mentioned this to her hair stylist. Sure enough, the stylist responded that her brother-in-law was one of the head accounting people in the company my client was interested in. The stylist asked for a business card to pass along to her brother-in-law and my client gladly complied. Less than a week later, my client got a call from the stylist's brother-in-law. This call resulted in an interview. After a series of interviews, my client is now happily employed at the company she targeted. The morals of the story: Network; spread the word; don't ignore any possible sources. Who would have thought that a contact with a hair stylist could lead to an accounting position in a major retail chain? But it did. If you've targeted specific companies you want to work for, don't hesitate to ask anyone you know if they know anyone inside that company.

Another obvious approach to get interviews with a targeted company is to simply find out who the hiring manager is for that company and then call them. If you're lucky, you'll be able to talk directly to the hiring manager. If not, you may have to go through the gatekeeper or the secretary to find out if there are any current openings. Even if there are no current openings, I encourage you to send a follow up note directly to the hiring manager and express your interest in working for the company. Ask them to contact you whenever there is an opening. And one other footnote: If there is a gatekeeper and you have a feeling that the gatekeeper is not forwarding your information to the hiring manager, you might try to call just before or soon after normal work hours before the gatekeeper arrives or before he or she leaves for the day. Many of my clients have found those before or after regular work hours to be the best times to reach hiring managers directly by phone.

And, whether you can't get past the gatekeeper or if the hiring manager tells you that there are no current openings, it's always important for you to follow up in some way, shape, or form, whether that's with a phone call or a personal "thanks for your time" note. Be persistent without becoming a nuisance. Your goal in any follow up should be to convey that you have sincere interest in interviewing with or working for that company and for you to create top-of-the-mind awareness as a possible candidate. This small gesture of following up can sometimes place you above other candidates when a job comes open.

Tips for Building a Resume that Can Get You Hired.

Your resume is likely to be a key element in determining whether or not you are able to secure an interview. In developing your resume, you should remember that it will often be compared side-by-side with the resumes of other candidates. With this in mind, you'll want to make sure that your resume stands out compared to these other resumes. Here are some basic tips which you can use in building a resume that will get you hired:

Before you build your own resume, you should review other sample resumes, which are very easy to find on the internet. If you are looking for a job in specific industries, I suggest that you also search industry-specific resumes to see what other people are doing in the same industry. (LinkedIn is a great place to view resumes of people within specific industries.)

After you've reviewed various sample resumes, you should then find out what standard resume templates are available. You can find resume templates by simply searching "free resume templates" on the internet. Also, as many of us have Microsoft Word, that software program has free resume templates available. Take a look at some of these templates and determine a template that will work for you.

One of the keys in developing any resume is to make it easy to read. This means that you should use a simple type style, such as Helvetica, Times Roman, Arial, or Calibri. Nothing too fancy. Type size should generally be 10 or 12 point type, nothing smaller. You should limit your resume to one or two pages, nothing longer. If you want to use color highlights and bold or italic type in some areas, you should feel free to do so, as long as you don't overuse these functions. I've received resumes before that were loaded with bold, capital letters, sometimes color-highlighted and underlined. In viewing these resumes, I've often felt that the sender is screaming at me, trying way too hard to get my attention.

Job Interview Preparation

In drafting your resume, you should remember that in most instances you'll be tweaking or adjusting each resume you send, depending on the job you are applying for. In customizing your resume for a particular job application, I encourage you to read the posting or description for the job and then make note of the keywords within that posting. Those keywords should give you a good idea as to what qualities or experience the employer is looking for in the employee they hire. You should then try to work some of these keywords into both your resume and your cover letter, without being too obvious. Also, if you are applying for a job at a larger company or a branch of a larger company, you should remember that many companies are now using a software bot to initially read your resume before it is passed along to a human. Some of these software bots are programmed to search for keywords. That's another reason why it's important to include the employer's keywords in your resume.

In listing information on your resume, also make a point to list important and relevant information first. In other words, if you're 40 years old, over 20 years removed from high school, you should not list your high school accomplishments near the top of your resume. List the experience, the accomplishments, the information which is most relevant to the job you are applying for. In listing your accomplishments, list numbers whenever possible. For example, if you had experience as a salesperson previously, instead of just saying that you were the salesperson for the North Central region, you might point out that you increased sales by 32% over the period of two years in the North Central region you were responsible for. Or, if you were on a salesforce of 13 people, and were the company's salesperson of the year, you need to make note of that. The more specific you can be,

Job Interview Preparation

the more your talents and accomplishments will resonate with the prospective employer.

Also, you should use active/powerful language whenever possible to outline your achievements. Words like "achieved", "earned", "accomplished", and "completed" are examples of power words which can be used to outline the achievements and accomplishments in your resume.

And make sure that your resume includes your contact information. (Phone number, email address, etc.) It's going to be hard for you to get an interview if the prospective employer doesn't know how to get a hold of you.

And finally, please proofread your resume and cover letter multiple times to make sure there are no typographical errors or other errors. I strongly suggest that you have other people check your resume for errors. Errors, especially typos, are totally unacceptable on resumes and I know hiring managers who will discard any resumes that have obvious errors. The feeling is that if you can't pay attention to detail with a resume or cover letter, then you might not be able to pay attention to detail in the job the employer is hiring for. If you don't know anyone who is capable of proofreading your resume and cover letter and if you can't do it yourself, then I suggest that you hire a freelance proofreader to do that for you. Upwork is a freelance site in which you would be able to hire a proofreader, for maybe $5 to $10. Fiverr is another company that is a platform for freelancers, including proofreaders.

Cover Letters: Why You Need One and How to Make Yours Irresistible.

Whereas resumes should contain "just the facts", cover letters offer you additional opportunities to make a "pitch" for the job. Cover letters allow you to expand on some of the facts you listed on your resume. They allow you the opportunity to express your sincere interest in the job opening and explain why you are a good fit for the job. Also, cover letters allow you to showcase some of your personality and to establish yourself as someone who stands out above the other candidates applying for the same job.

Some job applicants make the major mistake of ignoring the importance of the cover letter, thinking that the hiring manager won't take the time to read it. I can unequivocally tell you that cover letters do get read by prospective employers and you should never ignore their importance. You should compose a fresh cover letter for each job you apply for.

Here are some tips to consider in writing those cover letters:

First of all, you need to identify the person you are sending the cover letter to and list their name in the salutation of the letter. Letters addressed "To Whom it May Concern" or "Hiring Manager" are not going to cut it. Get the name and the correct spelling of the person who is doing the hiring, even if you have to make a phone call to get this information. If, by chance, you're not able to get a name for whatever reason, you should at least get the title of the person who is doing the hiring. (i.e.—Director of Marketing, Human Resources Director, Accounting Manager, etc.)

As you write your cover letter, make sure you go beyond your resume. If you're just going to repeat all of the information that is on your resume, then you're diminishing the purpose of the cover letter. If there's anything on your resume that you'd like to expand upon, the cover letter offers you the opportunity to do so. Although you won't want to take up your entire cover letter in expanding upon something on your resume, the cover letter allows you a brief opportunity to do that.

It will help if you can come up with a great opening line for your letter. Whether you have a great opening line or not, early in your cover letter you should cover why you think you are a good fit for the job which is open. As an example, here is an opening line from someone who is applying for a management position in a Barnes & Noble bookstore. "I was excited to find that you have an opening for a management position at Barnes & Noble. I've been a fan and loyal customer of Barnes & Noble for many years now and, with my previous management experience, I feel that I can bring a lot to the table as a Barnes & Noble manager." In this opening line, you'll note that the applicant expresses their interest and enthusiasm for the job that is open. They also establish themselves as someone who is familiar with the company and loves the concept. (It's hard to quickly dismiss someone who is a loyal customer, right?) And then, the applicant highlights that they have management experience and notes that she thinks she can become a valuable part of the Barnes & Noble team. And, she does that with a casual tone, without being ridiculously formal. In two sentences, she's accomplished a lot.

When you are writing your cover letter, it's important that you are aware of the keywords which the prospective employer has used in their job post. In the Barnes & Noble job post, the company had stated that it was looking for someone with management experience. As a result, the applicant was quick to mention her management experience in her cover letter. Another example would be if a prospective employer says they are looking to hire a committed employee who can be a valuable part of the team. The keywords here are "committed" and "team". With this in mind, your cover letter might mention that you are a hard worker and that you work well with others as part of a team. In reiterating the keywords from the job posting, you'll be reinforcing that you are a good fit for their job.

In your letter, you should explain why you are a better fit than any other people who are applying for the same position. If you're short on the experience or credentials they're asking for, then you're going to have to emphasize less tangible assets, such as positive attitude, work ethic, employee loyalty, etc. In doing this, I recommend that you do not point out or mention your lack of experience or credentials. Let the prospective employer discover this themselves. Instead of saying, "Although I don't have much experience....", you should say, "I am willing to work hard to become an invaluable member of the team" or "As my previous supervisor would tell you, I have a positive 'can do' attitude, I am a loyal employee, and I work well with others." Again, don't apologize for lack of experience or credentials. Identify the keywords in the job posting which apply to you and then highlight the attributes you have that correspond with those keywords. (If you don't fit with any or many of the keywords in the job posting, you may not be a good fit for the job.)

Also, in creating your cover letter, please remember to emphasize "what you can do for the company" instead of "what the company can do for you." The hiring manager already knows what the company can do for you. Your approach should be to tell them what you can bring to the table if they hire you. Hiring managers don't want to hear that their jobs will feed your family, allow you to get the sports car you've always wanted, or place you on the career path you want to be on. Instead, you need to highlight what you can do for them and their company.

And, similar to the recommendations made for resumes, if you get a chance to use numbers to illustrate your past successes, you should do so. (i.e.—"As sales manager for the Northeast Region, I increased sales by 65% the first year and 32% the second year.") Again, remember that hiring managers like numbers to illustrate past successes. Tangible assets are usually preferred over intangible assets in resumes and cover letters.

Cover letters also offer you the opportunities for testimonials, although you should again remember that cover letter space is somewhat limited. If you get the chance to use a testimonial, you should do so. (i.e.—"My supervisor told me that I had performed like a superhero in organizing that event", "One of my customers told me that the assistance I provided had 'saved the day' ", "I consistently received top reviews for my ability to guide our customer service team", etc.)

I strongly recommend that you keep your cover letters to one page only. And even though you should have listed your contact info on your resume, you should list the same contact info on your cover letter in case the resume and cover letter end up getting separated.

And, finally, another reminder for you to make sure that you have proofread your cover letter before sending. Typographical or grammatical errors could well eliminate you from consideration. If at all possible, use an additional set of eyes to proof your cover letter and your resume. Enlist the services of someone who is good at proofreading.

Job Interview Preparation

Chapter 2—Dress to Conquer

Okay, you've landed a face-to-face interview. What's next? Well, one of the things that is often overlooked is the decision on how to dress and what to wear for the interview. Although I've never been a "What to wear? What to wear?" person, as a career counselor I've seen applicants lose job opportunities based on the way they've dressed for an interview. With this in mind, here are some recommendations and suggestions on how you should dress for your interview.

What to Wear if You're a Man.

Unlike women's interview attire, men's interview attire is relatively straightforward. I always tell my male clients that, as an interviewee, their goal in regards to their attire should be not to stand out in an interview. If a man is standing out in an interview by the way he is dressed, it may well mean that the interviewer viewed his attire negatively. As a male, even though you certainly want to dress for success in any interview, your goal should simply be to fit in from an attire standpoint. Your ultimate goal should be to get the job based on what you say in the interview and what you have to offer, not on how you are dressed. If you think that a hiring manager is going to hire you based on the way you're dressed, unless you're applying for a job in the fashion industry, you're probably focusing on the wrong area. That being said, you can't disregard the importance of dressing for success and making a good impression based on the way you dress.

I'll never forget my first interview out of college. As a fresh-faced 21-year-old, I had the opportunity to interview for a public relations job with a major restaurant chain. At that time, many years ago, the company had all five selected candidates sit in the lobby at the same time as we waited to be interviewed. In sitting in the lobby with the other four applicants, it was immediately apparent that I was the kid fresh out of college and the other four candidates, also males, were older and experienced. I wore my only suit, my baby blue "interview suit", and a pair of spongy-soled dress shoes. The other candidates all wore more traditional attire, darker suits and more traditional shoes, including wingtips and penny loafers. I knew immediately that my interview attire would make me stand out from the other candidates, and not in a good way. But then again, I was less than a couple weeks out of college and I didn't know any better. I was fortunate enough to get invited back for a second interview for a job I really wanted. Again, as a kid right out of college, I was accustomed to wearing jeans and t-shirts every day and my "baby blue" interview suit was the only suit I owned. As I didn't want to wear the same suit to the second interview and I had no money to buy another suit, I borrowed my college roommate's suit for the second interview. Thankfully, we were about the same size; thankfully, I was offered the job despite my wardrobe deficiency. But I learned a lesson from that, and I made sure that I was dressed more appropriately for my subsequent interviews with other companies years later.

In determining what to wear for an interview, it will be helpful if you know what the dress code or dress mode is for the company you're interviewing with. Not all companies dress alike and you'll find that employees for a startup company are likely to dress different than employees who work for a corporate law firm. If you're not sure of what a particular company's dress code is, and you really want to make sure that you fit in when you are there for your interview, there's no harm in calling the receptionist at that company to find out how most people dress. I've even had clients who have gone to the company they were scheduled to interview with and, days before the interview,

Job Interview Preparation

scoped out how employees are dressed with a reconnaissance mission in the parking lot. Although I think this is a bit drastic, it does point out that it's important for you not to look too out of place with what you wear for your interview.

Hopefully, you'll know something about the company you sent your resume to and you'll have a feel for what kind of business they're in and how they might dress. If you're interviewing for the position of a golf pro or a landscaper, you can obviously dress very casual for your interview. As a matter of fact, you'd probably surely lose points if you showed up in a coat and tie. But for most other jobs, you may want to determine if the company you're interviewing with has business casual or business formal. The basic difference between these two modes of attire primarily deals with whether you should wear a tie or not, but also may deal with whether you should plan to wear a suitcoat or not.

Either way, I always tell my male clients that, if they're going to wear a coat, a khaki coat or camel-color coat is preferred over a darker coat. I tell clients not to dress like they would dress for going to a funeral. Pinstripe suits may be too formal, depending on the job you're applying for. Navy blazers may be more appropriate. Pants should obviously be coordinated with the coat. Navy, khaki, or even grey slacks are standard for most interviews. Whether you wear a tie or not may depend on whether you're going for the business casual or business formal look. Business casual is often without a tie, while business formal usually includes a tie.

If you're trying to straddle the line between business casual and business formal, a button-down shirt layered with a sweater is often acceptable attire, unless the sweater is the sweater you bought for an ugly sweater party. Again, whether you wear a tie will depend on whether you are going for the business casual or business formal look.

With your tie choice, you should select a tie that's not too bizarre, but it doesn't have to be boring either.

In choosing a button-down shirt, I recommend that you choose a solid color shirt or a pinstripe shirt, something that works with the other items you're going to wear and something that won't detract from the overall look. I recommend that you choose a long sleeve button-down over a short sleeve button-down, only because I know some people who are adverse to short sleeve button-downs for men.

Based on the rest of your interview attire, you should choose a nice pair of conservative shoes that works with the outfit. Nothing wrong with wearing brown shoes in conjunction with a business casual or business formal look. And make sure that your shoes are polished, certainly not scuffed. Also, a leather belt and conservative dark socks are normal interview attire for men, although with some of the unique and colorful sock designs today, patterned socks might work also.

And if you're a heavy jewelry wearer, go light on the jewelry unless you're applying for a job as a rap music producer. Joke. The same goes for cologne or after-shave. Go without or go very light.

And make sure your fingernails are clean and properly manicured.

What to Wear if You're a Woman.

It shouldn't surprise anyone when I say that deciding what to wear for an interview is often more complicated for women than it is for men. Although I'm going to spend more time on women's attire than I did for men's attire, I want to caution women and tell them not to overthink the attire you decide to wear to an interview. Although the way you dress in an interview is certainly important, it is still

Job Interview Preparation

secondary compared to preparing for the verbal parts of the interview itself.

How you dress for an interview will again depend on the type of company you're interviewing with. Dress codes for different companies can vary substantially. A startup company might allow jeans and tennis shoes, while a Fortune 500 Madison Avenue company might even discourage any attire that doesn't include a skirt and pantyhose. That's why it's important for you to find out what kind of dress code the company you're interviewing with has before you interview. Again, if you're not sure, you might simply call the company receptionist and ask about the dress code or standard attire. And, if you're still not sure, I would tell you that it's better to dress up instead of dressing down compared to the level of the employees there.

In most cases, I encourage women to dress conservatively. Nothing too flashy. Nothing too revealing in terms of top or skirt length. Normal conservative skirt length is just above or just below the knee. Select a conservative blouse or top that coordinates with your outfit.

Unlike men, accessories are more of a major factor for women. If you're a woman, you have to choose whether to wear jewelry or not. And, if you choose to wear jewelry, you'll have to choose what jewelry to wear. Also, you'll have to choose what bag to bring to an interview. In terms of jewelry, some people maintain that women should wear little or no jewelry to an interview. Either way, it's safe to say that you shouldn't overload the amount of jewelry you wear to an interview. I have a friend in the career counseling business who tells women that she would rather see them wear no jewelry at all instead of cheap jewelry. Also, in terms of the bag you choose to bring with you to an interview, the bag should be large enough to hold your resume and any corresponding paperwork, however it should not be one of those monstrous bags that we sometimes see. In my human resources days, I once had a woman that brought it bag so big into her interview that it took her at least five minutes to find her resume. In looking for her resume, she proceeded to empty her bag of its contents, piece by piece. By the time she finally located her resume, she could have had a garage sale with all the items she had placed on my desk, and, during that time, I had formed an opinion that she was disorganized. In other words, her chances of getting that job had ended even before the interview really got started.

Also, I encourage women to be cognizant of the amount of makeup and the perfume they wear. I would encourage women to go light on the makeup and to go without or go light on the perfume. It's important to remember that some people are allergic to perfumes and other people detest the heavy use of perfumes. With this in mind, the use of perfumes in an interview probably isn't a risk that's worth the reward.

Just as I advised men to make sure they had clean manicured nails, I encourage women to make sure their nails are presentable.

Clothes should be always be conservative, so as not to detract from the interview itself. The clothes themselves should be ironed and/or wrinkle-free. They should also be clean. No stains, holes, snags, or ragged edges. And beware of pet hair if you have a dog or cat.

Shoes should be polished and not scuffed. Whether you wear high heels or flats is up to you. Open-toe shoes are discouraged.

If you're going to a startup interview with a company that has a very casual dress code, jeans and tennis shoes may be OK, but the jeans should be clean and without holes and ragged seams. If you are interviewing with a company that has a very casual dress code, I strongly encourage you to make absolutely sure how casual it is before wearing jeans and tennis shoes to an interview. If you're wrong with that, your chance to get the job could be over before the interview starts. If you're not sure, then it's safer to dress up instead of taking the risk of dressing down.

Six Things You Should Not Wear to an Interview.

Although many of these things are common-sensical, there are some definite no-no's in what you should not wear or take to an interview.

1) Bright, flashy clothes. Try not to look like a decorated, walking Christmas tree. Stick with more conservative, solid colors. If you're going to wear a bright color, such as a bright red top, make sure that the rest of your outfit offsets or balances the bright colors you're wearing. Again, the goal here is for you not to stand out for the clothes you are wearing. You simply want to look polished and professional.

2) Scuffed, dirty, or outdated shoes. This tip applies to both men and women. You'd be surprised at how many people pay close attention to shoes and I'm presuming that hiring managers are included.

3) Too much jewelry or too many accessories. If you're a man, take off the bling or tuck it inside your shirt. If you're a woman, no large dangling earrings. And if you wear funky eyeglasses, go back to your more conventional and conservative design, at least for purposes of the interview.

4) Outlandish ties, scarves, socks. This applies particularly to men, but also to women who accessorize with scarves. If

you're a man, don't try to be the funny guy with an outlandish tie or socks. You're not there to enhance your future as a standup comic. If you are a bow tie wearer, you might consider a more conventional necktie. Although I think bow ties can be quite fashionable, you should know that some people still have an aversion to them.

5) Heavy makeup; heavy perfume or colon. Instead of wearing heavy makeup, or heavy perfume or cologne, I'd recommend that you either go light or go without. Some people are allergic to perfumes or colognes; other people are very sensitive to scents. You never know if one of the people you meet in an interview with be of the same kind. Also, go light on the makeup. Don't overdo it. Avoid bright red lipstick and dark eyeshadow. A light coat of mascara, a touch of powder, and some tinted lip balm are probably OK, but don't overdo it.

6) Outdated or worn bags, portfolios, briefcases. Some people totally forget about the bags or briefcases they use to carry their resume or interview paperwork. Make sure that the vessel you're using is presentable and professional, and conveys the image you want to present to your prospective employer. If you're a woman with a bag, choose a smaller size bag and minimize the contents so you can easily find the paperwork you'll need during your interview. And always bring a pen.

Again, with any of these recommendations, you should know that they're not set in concrete. I always encourage people to be who they are and to dress accordingly. However, in choosing what to wear and how you want to look for an interview, always keep in mind the person or persons you might be meeting during the

Job Interview Preparation

interview and consider what kind of impression you're making with the way you're dressed or accessorized.

The Truth About Tattoos and Piercings.

So, you have some tattoos or some piercings. Well, you're certainly not alone. Almost 30% of Americans have tattoos and half of all millennials have tattoos. That being said, you're probably aware that some people still have some biases or negative feelings about tattoos and piercings and, with this in mind, you may have to decide how you're going to handle that going into an interview.

First of all, let me point out that with some jobs and some employers, it's not going to matter at all whether you have tattoos or piercings. However, some other companies may even have company policies in place regarding tattoos and piercings.

Before we discuss how you should handle tattoos and piercings going into an interview, I'd like to provide you with some additional information which may help you in your decision on how to handle. A popular survey site recently revealed the results of a survey they did regarding tattoos and piercing. They asked respondents if they felt that tattoos and piercings hurt an applicant's chances of getting a job. 76% of respondents felt that tattoos and piercings did indeed hurt an applicant's chances in getting a job. Along the same lines, over 37% of the people surveyed said that they felt that employees with tattoos and piercings reflected poorly on their employers. 42% thought that visible tattoos were inappropriate at work; 55% felt that piercings were inappropriate at work.

In looking at these survey results, there's no denying that there is still a lot of bias against tattoos and piercings, whether that's fair or not. It should be pointed out that peoples' age is a significant factor in how tattoos and piercings are perceived. As you might guess, older age groups have a more negative perception of tattoos and piercings; younger age groups are more accepting.

People who have negative perceptions of tattoos and piercings are prone to think that people who have these tattoos and piercings are, among other things, less intelligent (27% of respondents thought that people with tattoos and piercings were less intelligent than people without tattoos and piercings, less attractive (45%), and more rebellious (50%). Unfortunately, the perceptions of women with tattoos and piercings are even worse than the perceptions of men. Whereas some people perceive men with tattoos as being more masculine, more dominant, and more aggressive, women with tattoos are perceived to be less honest, less motivated, less generous, and less creative, among other things. Those negative perceptions are most certainly an unfair burden to bear for a qualified candidate. I list these seemingly unfair assumptions only so you can see what perceptions you're dealing with if you're someone that has tattoos or piercings. You may be a perfectly qualified candidate for a job position, but you may be stigmatized or categorized because you have tattoos or piercings.

In deciding whether you should hide your tattoos in an interview or to allow them to be seen, here are some possible factors:

1) Consider the industry and the position you are applying to. If you're going to be face to face with customers in that position, you may well have to cover your tattoos and ditch the piercings. Positions such as face-to-face customer service representatives, retail sales people, and bank tellers are all positions in which you're going to be working with the public on an ongoing basis and, as a result, your

employer may not allow you to have your tattoos and piercings visible.

2) Research and consider the company culture. As mentioned before, some companies even have company policies against tattoos and piercings. If they do, you're going to have to make a decision on how important it is for you to exhibit your tattoos and piercings, both in the interview and on the job, if you get the job. If you're adamant about not hiding your tattoos or piercings and if the company you're interested in has a policy against tattoos or piercings, you should know that this may impact your interest in working for that company or their interest in hiring you. In other words, it may be a dealbreaker.

3) Hide them in the interview and then ask later. If you're not sure what the company stance is on tattoos and piercings going into the interview, it's probably best to hide them (if possible) for the interview. If you have tattoos on your arms that can be simply covered with a long sleeve shirt, then cover them for the interview and if it appears that the interviewer has further interest in you as a candidate, you can always ask him or her if there is a company policy regarding tattoos or piercings. If you have tattoos that can't be covered, such as tattoos on your fingers or the side of your face, you'll certainly have to broach that in the interview as it's unlikely that you'll be able to cover your face or your hands in most of the jobs you apply for. Whenever I discuss tattoos in this chapter, please know that I'm presuming that the tattoos you have are not offensive.

Job Interview Preparation

If you have tattoos that are going to be offensive to co-workers or customers, that's a whole different scenario and you may well find that those tattoos may prohibit you from getting a job and you may have to have them altered or removed before you can get a job.

4) Don't let your tattoos or piercings be a distraction in an interview. When you interview for a job, you're hopefully going to want your talents and abilities to be the main determinants as to whether you get the job or not. With this in mind, you won't want your tattoos or piercings to be a distraction in the interview. Getting a great job can be difficult enough without having your tattoos detract from the reasons you're the right person for the job.

In summary, please know that I always encourage people to be themselves when they interview. I can't tell you whether you should hide your tattoos or piercings or whether you should allow them to be visible. You'll have to make that decision yourself. However, I did want to arm you with some information and remind you that some people still have a bias against and a negative perception of tattoos and piercings. Depending on the company you're interviewing with and the position you're applying for, you'll have to determine whether exhibiting your tattoos and piercings will inhibit your chances to get a job that you're interested in. And you'll also have to determine whether the tattoos or piercings would prohibit you from doing the job itself. If the company has a policy against visible tattoos, are you going to be willing to cover your tattoos every day? If you're really interested in the job and you don't have a problem with hiding your tattoos and dissing your piercings, then I recommend that you hide them during the interview. Then if you and the prospective employer have further interest in the opening, you should find out what company policy is toward displaying these markings.

Chapter 3—Prepare Like a Boss

In preparing for an interview, it's important that you prepare for that interview as much as possible. Preparation is a great way for you to overcome any anxiety you might have going into an interview. If you've prepared properly, you'll give yourself the best chance to land the job.

How to Overcome Anxiety and Nervousness.

First of all, let me tell you that it's normal to feel nervous or have some butterflies going into an interview. After all, that interview may well hold the key to your future and you shouldn't ignore the fact that it could provide the next step for you in your career or your livelihood. So, don't let the fact that you have some anxiety alarm you. It's natural.

With this section of the book, I'm going to give you some suggestions on how you can conquer your anxiety as you prepare for the interview and also in the interview itself. Most of my suggestions will revolve around preparation. If you prepare adequately for your interview, you'll give yourself the chance to ace the interview and land a job offer.

My first recommendations involve eating and sleeping. You should make sure you're well rested before you head into an interview. Get a good night of sleep. Also, lay off the caffeine, as it will only increase your anxiety. No caffeinated coffee, no caffeinated soft drinks. And, obviously don't drink alcohol before an interview. This includes not drinking too much the night before the interview. I also suggest that you eat something or have a light snack before going into an interview. I had a client who went into an interview with an empty stomach and, as a result, her stomach was growling loudly throughout the interview. She was so embarrassed that she couldn't focus on the interview. In a similar horror story, I had another client who ate a greasy meal before his interview and, as a result, he had to ask to use the restroom in the middle of the interview. Along the same lines, I've also had clients tell me that the heavy meals they ate before interviews made them sleepy during the interview. So, bottom line is that you need to pay attention to what you eat and drink prior to an interview.

Another way to reduce anxiety for your interview will be to make sure you arrive on time, presuming it's a face-to-face interview. If you arrive just before an interview, you may increase your anxiety. If you arrive late, you may be eliminated from the job opportunity before the interview even starts. And, if by chance, you find out that you're going to be late for the interview, you need to call the person you were supposed to meet with and tell them you will be late. You'd be surprised how many people show up late for interviews without informing the person they're meeting with. If you're not exactly sure how to get to the location where the interview is being held, make sure you find out how to get there. Use Mapquest or one of the other internet sites to get driving directions or use the GPS system on your phone to guide you and make sure that you allow time for possible traffic delays. If weather is an issue and is creating poor driving conditions, I suggest that you contact the interviewer before you even set out to drive there; then keep them posted on your progress if anything changes as you work your way toward their location. If the job is important enough to you, and the location isn't too far from you, I've had clients who've made trial runs in the days before the interview. But if you're doing a trial run, make sure you're accounting for the time of day and the different traffic levels during the time of day. I've had clients who did their trial runs during non-business hours and then when they travelled to their interview location during rush hour, the transit time was much longer and they found they hadn't allowed enough transit time.

Another way to reduce interview anxiety is to plan what you're going to wear ahead of time, at least a day ahead of time. I've had clients who have waiting until the morning of the interview to decide what they were going to wear for an interview, only to find that the suitcoat they planned to wear had a stain on it or was loaded with pet hair, the shirt or blouse they planned to wear had more wrinkles than a Sharpei, or the shoes they planned to wear needed polishing. If you're running around trying to plan your wardrobe on the day of the interview, you'll most certainly be increasing your anxiety.

It's also important that you do your homework regarding the company you're interviewing with, especially if you're not familiar with them. The internet offers all of us the chance to research companies from our living rooms. If you haven't visited the web site of the company you'll be interviewing with, you need to do so. Also, please use Google or another search engine to see if there are any recent news articles that provide information on the company. I had a client who, when researching the company she was going to interview with, found out that the company was having some serious financial issues that she hadn't been aware of. Although this information didn't discourage her from proceeding with the interview, it certainly gave her some questions to ask during the interview. Another way to learn about the companies you are interviewing with is to solicit personal information. Do you know someone who works for that company or worked for them in the past? Do you know someone who works for a competitor of the company you're interviewing with? In soliciting personal information and even with searching for information on the internet, I

Job Interview Preparation

always caution people to take their findings with "a grain of salt". The information you receive could be inaccurate or tainted, but nevertheless it should at least give you some food for thought and possibly some information or questions that will help you in your interview.

Another way for you to reduce your anxiety is to prepare for the actual interview itself. First, make sure you have all the necessary materials to take with you to the interview: resume, copy of your cover letter, reference list, portfolio with samples of your work, certifications, licenses, business cards, and certainly a pen and notepad. Again, pay attention to detail with the materials you gather. No coffee or soda stains on your resume, no pens that you or your dog have chewed, etc. You get the picture.

Also, in preparing for an interview, you can reduce your anxiety by determining some of the questions you want to ask before the interview. If you think there's a chance you won't remember the questions you want to ask, write them down on a sheet of paper and take that with you to the interview.

Do you have a friend or relative who you can practice the interview with? If so, you might find that conducting a mock interview will be very helpful. Give your friend some questions to ask you based on the questions you think you'll be asked during the interview itself. People who do mock interviews prior to their actual interviews seem to benefit immensely from the practice of formulating and giving answers to possible questions. There's no doubt that this practice boosts confidence heading into the interview.

As you head into an interview, you may find it beneficial to "step outside yourself" and the thoughts of the interview itself. Some people find this extremely helpful, as they relish every part of the interview process. They greet and engage the receptionist, they say a brief hello to any people they pass along the way to the interview room, they ask the interviewer how his or her day is going, they focus on remembering the names of the people they meet, they focus on a firm handshake and eye-to-eye contact, etc. In other words, they break each part of the interview process into a separate event and, as a result, it's much easier for them to relax and cast off any anxiety they might be feeling.

In the interview itself, I always encourage people to "slow down". When we get anxious, we tend to rush things and that can lead to undesirable results. I have a friend who is a youth basketball coach and during big moments of the games when his players may be experiencing anxiety, he always tells them to slow down. The same goes with interviews. If you have anxiety and the interviewer asks you a question, instead of blurting out the answer, slow down and take some time and think about how you want to answer the question. That should be helpful in reducing your anxiety.

Along the same lines, you should note that some interviewers will try to catch applicants off-guard by grilling them or interrogating them. For applicants with anxiety, this can really throw them off track. If this happens to you, you should understand why the interviewer may be doing this and you should also understand that he or she is probably using the same tack with other candidates. Interviewers will sometimes grill candidates in order to find out how the candidate will react to stress. If you know in advance that this is an approach used by some interviewers, you'll feel a lot less anxiety knowing what the motivation is and knowing that all candidates are probably being handled in the same manner.

And finally, another way to reduce your anxiety in an interview is to ask the interviewer some questions and let them answer. "Throw the ball in their court", in other words. Hopefully, you'll have some questions prepared in advance and you'll also be able to formulate other questions throughout the interview. You'll find that you'll have a much better chance to land the job if you can turn the interview from a monologue into a two-way conversation. Not only will you have less anxiety, you may well find that the interview feels much better about the interview if it is a conversation instead of an interrogation.

Nine Things You Need to Research for Your Interview.

Research is a huge part of the preparation for any interview. If you want to give yourself the best chance to land the job, you'll make sure that you've researched the job you're applying for and the corresponding company.

1) About the Company. You'd be surprised how many job applicants don't know much about the company they're interviewing with. When the interviewer asks what you know about the company and you respond, "Well, my brother-in-law told me it's a great place to work", that's not going to cut it. You'll actually have to know something more about the company you're hoping to work for. The internet and Google make it very easy for job applicants to research companies. Almost all companies have web sites and you can learn a lot about companies by browsing their web sites. You can generally glean recent news items, company history, and even company culture from a web site. Most web sites have an About Us page that will impart some information about the company. Some web sites will have links to their blogs or newsletters. You can learn a lot about most companies in perusing this information. By the same token, I would also use Google to uncover additional information about the company

you'll be interviewing. You should remember that sometimes company websites provide a rosy picture of the company that is contrary to what you might find in searching articles or reviews on Google. Again, I should remind you to be prepared to take this information "with a grain of salt". For example, if you are interested in working for a certain restaurant and you find an article trashing that restaurant on Google, take that article with a grain of salt. It could be an instance in which someone is on a crusade and has an axe to grind against that restaurant. On the other hand, if you see repeated complaints against that restaurant or any other company, you can probably presume that they have a problem in that area.

2) Corporate/Company Culture. If you read between the lines on the company web site or in the company blogs or newsletters, you should be able to get a feel for the corporate culture. If a newsletter describes the company's annual picnic and shows lots of families with kids, that might mean that it's a company that values its employees and their families. If a company is involved in a lot of outside charitable activities (raising money for the local children's hospital, building and repairing homes as part of Habitat for Humanity, etc.), then you can presume that the company culture includes charitable work in the community. If the newsletters refer to company softball teams, corporate outings, or corporate planning sessions or retreats, you have an additional glimpse into the culture of the company. You can also find out more about a company and its culture by viewing their social media accounts, including platforms such as Facebook, Twitter, Instagram, and LinkedIn.

Job Interview Preparation

3) Company History. It's good if you can gather some information about the history of the company. Maybe you'll find out that the company was started by a couple of college buddies in a dorm room or that a company's first fast food restaurant was started in Southern California. Whatever information you find may give you a better indication of where the company came from and how that relates to what it is now. And don't hesitate to "drop" some of the information you learn into your interview conversation whenever appropriate. It won't hurt your chances if the interviewer knows that you took some time to do your homework.

4) The Key Players. In researching a prospective employer, you should determine who the key players are. Whether that is the founder, the owner, the current CEO, or various department heads, it will behoove you to find out what you can about the company's key players. As an example, I have a client of mine who has been on a career track in restaurant marketing for a couple of decades now. When he researches the next company he would like to work for, one of the first things he does is to check to see what the backgrounds of the key players are. Do they all have restaurant backgrounds or do some of them have non-restaurant backgrounds? Are the key players mostly young or are they older? In reading the bios of one of his recent target companies, my client determined that two of the company bigwigs had the same college alma mater as he did. He also found that a number of them were heavy into golfing as a hobby. My client made a note of this, as he was also an avid golfer. And later on, when the opportunity presented itself, he mentioned his love for golf in an interview and it led

Job Interview Preparation

to a conversational discussion with the hiring manager, who was also an avid golfer. Bottom line is that my client researched the key players of the company he was interested in working for and he used the information he gained to his advantage, finding common ground with the person who did the interviewing and some of the company's key executives. With the knowledge that his alma mater was the same as a couple of the executives and that one of his favorite pastimes was the same as some of the corporate executives, he was able to establish common ground and give them the indication that he would fit in with the company and its executives.

5) The Interviewer. Hopefully, you can get the name of the person who will be interviewing you and you can then do some quick research on them. If the interviewer is not listed on the company web site, you can certainly check social media platforms and Google to see if you can find a presence. Again, you don't want to go overboard with this, however you might be able to find "common ground" between you and your interviewer with the information you are able to find.

6) Company Competitors. Most companies have competitors and it may be useful for you to find out who those competitors are and how those competitors might affect the company's position.

7) News, Recent Events. Part of this should probably be under the About the Company section, but it's also important enough to have its own section or mention. You can use the internet to find out all kinds of information about the company you'll

be interviewing with. Recent news articles, blogs, or newsletters might tell you about new products they're introducing, new services they're offering, a new branch or location they're opening, their expansion into other countries, etc. As some of this news may relate to the job opening you're applying for, this information might be extremely helpful to you in determining why the company has the opening.

8) Reviews. Just as you search for news and information on the company you'll be interviewing with, you should also check reviews. This can often by simply done in Google by listing the name of the company and then listing the word "reviews" behind it. (i.e.—XYZ reviews). You might be surprised by what you find in reviews. For example, my neighbor's son was looking for a summer job between his first and second year of college. He wanted to work retail and he had a specific retail chain in mind. Before he sent his application to the company he had wanted to target, he searched reviews for this company online. He was surprised to find out that the company he had been interested in was notorious for paying its employees less than many other retail concepts and a number of reviews from ex-employees revealed some reasons why it probably wasn't the great place to work that he thought it might be. So, in his particular situation, researching reviews turned out to be very helpful for this young man and he ended up working for another higher-paying retailer.

9) Inside Scoop. Along the same lines as the abovementioned reviews, you can get additional scoops on prospective employers by searching the internet. Glassdoor.com is a site

that can provide inside information regarding many companies. The information provided includes salary figures, employee functions, company reviews, the hiring process, and other details you can use to your advantage in positioning yourself above other candidates for the same job.

Again, I'd like to emphasize the importance of doing your homework in researching prospective employers. In doing so, you're looking to find information which will place you above the other candidates looking to land the same job. In researching prospective employers, I always remind clients not to ignore seemingly unimportant information. As mentioned above in some of the previous examples, you might be able to use inconsequential information such as college alma maters or love of golf as a pastime to establish common ground with the person you're interviewing with or the company you want to work for. At the worst, you'll at least be able to show your prospective employer that you've taken the time to research their company. At the best, the information you find might be a keystone in helping you show that you're a good fit for the job you're applying for.

Other Vital Ways to Prepare for Your Job Interview.

Here are some additional tips you can use to prepare for your job interview:

Make sure you practice your answers to common interview questions. Most interviews contain the "Tell Me About Yourself" question in some shape or form, so you should definitely have an answer prepared to that question. A commonly asked question which has been the downfall of many job applicants, is the "Describe Your Biggest Weakness" question. This is a difficult question which needs to be handled properly. You probably won't want to say that you don't

Job Interview Preparation

have any weaknesses, as that may come off as cocky or arrogant. And you won't want to spend a lengthy time describing your weaknesses, as you'll certainly be better served by spending time on your strengths. When my clients ask me how they should handle this question, I tell them to list a specific weakness, but then to also explain how they are working to overcome the weakness. For example, I have a client who is somewhat shy, at least until people get to know him. He's in a public relations position, so his jobs have often entailed speaking in front of groups of people. He's never been comfortable with this, however he's worked to become proficient at it. So, when the interviewer asked him what his biggest weakness is, he replied, "I've never really been comfortable speaking in front of groups. However, I've worked hard at it. I've joined Toastmasters and I've offered myself as a guest speaker or guest presenter at various industry functions. I'm now to the point where I am much more comfortable speaking in front of groups, and I'm still working to get better, but I've improved considerably since I realized that I had some shortcomings as a public speaker. I'm to the point now where I no longer consider it to be a weakness."

Another question you're likely to get in one form or another is, "Why are you interested in this position?" or "Why are you interested in working for our company?" Again, you should have a rehearsed and polished answer to this question. In answering the question, it's important to emphasize what you can do for the company and what you can bring to the table instead of what the company can do for you.

In preparing for an interview, I strongly suggest that you practice answering different questions that might be asked. And practice your answers out loud. It's one thing to have an answer inside your head, but it's another thing to hear how that answer sounds when you express it vocally. I have a client who tells me that he sometimes practices his

Job Interview Preparation

answers in the shower, instead of singing. Other people will stand in front of mirrors as they practice answering questions. If you have a friend or relative, or even a loyal dog, who will volunteer to be a willing listener as you practice your answers, that will be even better. I've seen the results that mock interviews and practicing answers can produce and I strongly recommend that you include this in your interview preparation arsenal.

I also encourage people to prepare some questions to answer during the interview. And then, hopefully during the interview, you'll be able to come up with some additional questions to ask of your interviewer. It's OK to jot these questions down on a notepad and bring them with you to the interview. But make sure you stay engaged in the interview and listen to the information the interviewer is providing. You don't want to be asking questions for information the interviewer has already provided.

I also tell people to prepare an interview kit to take to the interview. This includes resumes, a copy of your cover letter, a copy of the job posting, samples of previous work you'd like to show, licenses and certifications, and a vetted reference listed. When I say vetted, I'm strongly suggested that you've already compiled a list of personal and professional references who you've contacted and who have agreed to vouch for you. You'd be surprised how many people list references without even informing them that they've been listed as a reference.

Your interview kit should include at least five or six resumes, as you can never be sure how many people you will meet during the interview process. And don't forget to include things such as paper napkins or tissues, breath mints or breath spray, a stain stick, a lint remover, and even an umbrella. In other words, be prepared.

Job Interview Preparation

If you're going to take a bag to your interview, make sure it's cleaned out and you're taking only the essentials you'll need for the interview. If you need someone to help you to carry your bag into the interview room because it's so heavy, you haven't cleaned it out enough. Joke.

And always bring a notebook and pen with you to the interview. That notebook can include any notes or questions you have prepared for the interview, but you can also use it to take notes and write down any questions you have throughout the interview process. Again, it's important that if you're going to take notes during an interview, don't overdo it. You won't want to spend all your time looking down at your notepad when you should be making eye contact and engaging with the interviewer. With the notes you bring into any interview, you should be familiar enough with those notes so you don't have to constantly refer to them. And you certainly don't want to read those notes verbatim. I also tell clients to pretend that they are a television newscaster, looking down at their notes occasionally, but spending almost all their time looking at and engaging with the interviewer. And yes, eye contact is extremely important. When you meet someone and when you interview with someone, you need to look them in the eye. When I was a hiring manager, I viewed this as an absolute must. Persons who didn't look me in the eye when I first met with them had already lost points with me.

Body language is important. Stand up straight, sit up straight, and act interested. No slouching or slumping.

Finally, if you're a person for whom conversation or speech doesn't flow smoothly, I suggest that you come up with a go-to phrase that you can use to fill space while you are forming your answers to any interview questions. Some people will simply repeat the question. i.e.—When asked why they're interested in working for the company they're interviewing with, they'll use that question to transition into their answer. "Why am I interested to work for the XYZ Company? Well, among other things, I love the industry and, with my experience and my enthusiasm, I think I could bring a lot to the table." Or, you could respond by saying, "That's a great question. I'd have to say that among the reasons I'd like to work for XYZ Company are the fact that…" You get the picture. If conversation or answering questions doesn't come easy for you, use some go-to phrases to fill the void while you gather your thoughts.

If you want to give yourself the best chance of acing your interview, you should make sure that you prepare for it. In most instances, you'll be competing for jobs against candidates who will certainly do their homework in preparing for the interview. You'll have to make sure that you can match or exceed their efforts if you're going to land the job for which you're interviewing.

Chapter 4—Questions and Answers

Going into an interview, you can never be sure what kinds of questions you're going to be asked. To help you with this process, I'm going to use my experience as a career counselor and give you both some common questions and some more difficult and challenging questions you might be asked in your interviews. Although I won't be able to give you the exact questions you'll be asked, the questions I've outlined should give you a good idea of what you might be asked in an interview.

12 Common Interview Questions and How to Ace Them.

Along with the common questions you might be asked, I've listed some tips on how you might answer. Although you'll obviously want to provide your own answers, the tips I've provided should give you some ideas on how you might answer the questions.

1) *"Tell me about yourself."* This is a very commonly asked question, often used near the start of an interview. With this request, the interviewer is trying to get a quick overview of who you are and make sure you're a good fit for the job opening. If you prepare to answer any common interview question, this is the question that you should most definitely practice answering, again and again. It's an important question and since it will almost always appear near the start of any interview, you'll want to immediately try to establish yourself as a formidable candidate; preferably as a candidate who stands

above the other candidates. In answering the question, you should provide an overview of your current position and then provide information as to how your current position is relative to the position you're applying for. Also, provide any other highlights from your career or background that relate to the job you're applying for. And, it's OK for you to include a few personal details that might help the interviewer to remember you and to separate you from the other candidates. i.e.—"And when I'm not working, I love to spend time with my family. This summer I'm coaching my nine-year-old daughter's softball team. I love it."

2) *"How would you describe yourself?"* When they ask this question, they're not looking for your height, your weight, and your eye color. Provide an answer that coincides with the qualities and abilities they said they're looking for in their job description. If one of the keywords in their job posting referred to someone who can lead a team of employees, you should then make sure that you mention that you are an excellent leader, someone who communicates well, enjoys leading a team, and is good at it. If their job post mentions that they are looking for someone who can take a project from start to finish without a lot of supervision, mention the fact that you can take a project and run with it in your answer. Offer only positive descriptions; try to correlate the description of yourself with the qualities they appear to be looking for in a candidate.

3) *"Why do you want to work here?"* This question offers a chance for you to show that you've done your homework and your research. With your answer, you can point out how the

Job Interview Preparation

company products, services, history, or culture relates to your interests. For example, when my college student daughter applied for a seasonal position in a bookstore, she was asked this question and she responded in kind: "I love books, I love bookstores, I love telling people about good books, and I love helping people. I've loved coming here as a customer with my parents from the time I was a little girl and I like the way this place makes customers feel like they're valued and welcome. The people who work in this store are always so helpful. I want to be one of those people." In my opinion, this was a terrific answer, as it told exactly why she wanted to work there. Admittedly, she was applying for a basic retail position, so she didn't get into a lot of specifics as to what she could bring to the table other than a "can-do" helpful attitude, but she's a college student and doesn't have a lot of work experience. If you're applying for a higher-level position, you can use more tangible and less emotional references on why you want to work there.

4) *"What interests you most about the job you're applying for?"* This question offers you the opportunity to tell how your skills, your experience, or your attitude match up with what they are looking for. Again, I'll remind you that you should think about what you can offer the company with this answer instead of what they can offer you.

5) *"Why are you looking to leave your current job?"* In answering this question, this is not the time to bash your current company or your current position. It's not time to pull out the crying towel or the axe to grind. Don't focus on the

negative aspects of your current company or position. Instead, focus on the opportunities or the positives that new job would offer you.

6) *"What are you passionate about?"* Another opportunity to relate your interests and passions to what the prospective employer is looking for. Again, go back to the original job posting and add any other information you've learned about the position you're interviewing for and formulate an answer that shows how your interests and passions fit with what they're looking for in an employee.

7) *"What are your greatest strengths?"* Here's a chance for you to toot your own horn. Again, your answer should relate to the qualities they're looking to find in a new employee. For example, if they are looking for someone who can create and implement new product introductions, you might respond, "I love developing new product campaigns and I'm good at it. I've done it at my current company and our product rollouts have always been very successful. I can take an introduction from the idea stage to the implementation stage and I can do that without much supervision. I consider myself to be an expert in developing product introductions and I think that's definitely something I can bring to the table in the position you're offering."

8) *"What are your greatest weaknesses?"* We outlined this question in detail earlier in this book, but I will again remind you that this is a bit of a trap question, as you won't want to spend a lot of time focusing on your deficiencies when you'll

Job Interview Preparation

be better served focusing on your strengths. It probably won't be wise for you to answer that you don't have any weaknesses, as that will likely come across as cocky and arrogant. So, with the answer you give, you will ideally give an example of a legitimate weakness that you have, but then you'll tell the interviewer how you have worked to correct this weakness. Are you a person who can't say "no" and takes on too much? If so, you might note with your answer that you've learned to say "no", you've learned to delegate, or you've learned to ask for help from your team. Are you someone who prefers to do things yourself instead of delegating it to a fellow employee who might not be able to do it as well? If so, explain how you've worked to bridge this weakness. Maybe you've made a more concentrated effort to educate the employee at the start of the project or maybe you meet with the employee a couple times a week throughout the project to make sure that they're progressing as planned. Either way, whatever weakness you unveil to the interviewer, you should make sure you tell them how you've worked to rectify that deficiency.

9) *"What are your goals for the future?/Where do you want to be in five years?"* I'm not a big fan of these questions, but they're often asked nonetheless. In asking either of these questions, a hiring manager is most likely doing one of two things: They're probably trying to find out if you plan to stick around for a while or they want to find out how their company or their position fits into your long-term goals. So, in answering the question, you should again relate how their company and the job they are offering will fit into your plans. If you're interviewing for a restaurant marketing position and tell the interviewer that you want to own a tree trimming company in

the next five years, that's probably not going to help you secure the job you're interviewing for. Along the same lines, your answer should never be, "I have no idea." It's doubtful that your prospective employer is going to be interested in hiring an employee who has no idea where he is going with his life.

10) *"Tell me about a difficult work situation you've had and how you handled it?"* With this question, the interviewer is probably trying to determine how you handle adversity and/or to determine if you are able to solve problems. In answering a question like this, you should remember that stories are often more effective than facts and figures. If you have a story you can tell to show how you solved a difficult situation, it will be more memorable that any facts and figures you can relay. i.e.—An events planner has a wedding photographer cancel on her the day of the wedding… A major corporate client announces that he is thinking of taking his business elsewhere because he doesn't feel like he's been getting the proper amount of attention from the salesperson who works for you…You worked in a retail store during the holiday season, the line at the register was about 10 deep, and you had a customer who was loudly complaining about the wait. With any of these situations or your own difficult situation, you should detail how you worked to solve the problem. And, hopefully, it had a happy ending. And, ideally, this problem will relate in some way to the position you're applying for.

11) *"Why should we hire you?"* This is a question that normally appears near the end of the interview. If you get this question, you should consider it a final opportunity for you to reiterate what you can bring to the table and why you'll be a good fit for the job they're offering. Detail again the skills and experience which make you a great candidate to fill the open position. Also, don't be afraid to throw in a more emotional, less tangible statement, such as "I'm sure I'll be a valuable employee", "I assure you that I'll work hard to accomplish the goals you set for me", "I'm very interested in working here and I'm sure I can be a valued member of the team", etc.

12) *"Do you have any questions?"* This question also often appears at or near the end of the interview. It's not a throwaway question and you should never not have any additional questions. This question offers you the opportunity to cover any subjects which were not covered in the interview. Again, you should refer to any questions you had on your notepad before the interview or any questions that may have developed over the course of the interview. If all of your questions have been covered, take the opportunity to turn the remaining interview time into more of a conversation. You could ask the interviewer about their own experiences within the company, ask them what success would look like in the position they are hiring for, or ask them what are some of the challenges you might expect in the role they are hiring for. Either way, don't pass on an opportunity to show the interviewer that you're interested in the job they're offering by asking some pertinent questions. If you don't ask any

questions, the interviewer may not think that you're interested in the position.

Navigating Difficult Questions Like a Champion.

Don't be surprised if you are asked some difficult or challenging questions in your interview. After all, an interview is part of an elimination process and interviewers are looking for ways to separate the competition and determine who the best fit for the job will be.

When I was fresh out of college, I had an interview for a job I really wanted. I prepared diligently for that interview. I practiced answers to lots of different questions by enlisting my friends to conduct mock interviews. Over and over again, I rehearsed the answers to any questions I thought the interviewer might ask. By the time the interview rolled around, I thought that I was ready for just about any question imaginable. About three minutes into the interview, the interviewer asked me a question that left me totally off balance. Her question was, "If you were a tree, what kind of tree would you be and why?" Oops, I hadn't practiced for that one. Why in the world would an interviewer ask a question like that? I didn't have a lot of time to analyze why she asked me that, but I wanted to know what the method to her madness was in asking me that, before I gave my answer. I quickly determined, correctly I think, that she wanted to see if I was able to think outside the box and to see how my thought process was. After stuttering and stammering for just a short time, I replied, "I would be an oak tree. Oak trees are strong and steady and they're useful. Oak trees have a strong root system. When they're in full bloom, they provide shade for others to enjoy. And they provide nuts (acorns) that squirrels, chipmunks, wild turkeys, and other animals can enjoy." By the time I finished answering that question, I was confident that I handled it adequately.

Job Interview Preparation

Although there probably wasn't a right or wrong answer to that question, I was happy that I'd been able to provide some decent reasons why I would be an oak tree. I later joked that I was glad that I hadn't said I want to be a weeping willow tree or a sappy maple tree.

A client of mine reports that he was recently asked a similar question in an interview: "If you could be a superhero, what superhero would you be and why?" Again, I'm guessing that the interviewer was trying to determine the applicant's thought process with a question like this. My client, who told me that he really doesn't know of many superheroes, told me that he answered that he would be Batman, as Batman and Superman were the only two superheroes he could think of when he was asked the question. He said that he chose Batman because Batman is/was someone who is very protective. He works well with his associates, including his sidekick Robin and his butler Alfred. He is physically and mentally fit, and intelligent. He has a passion for justice and an interest in protecting people from injustice. My client then added that he was like Batman in that he works well with his co-workers, he tries to stay physically and mentally fit, and, as a loyal employee, he always wants to make things right if they're wrong.

Not a bad answer from my friend, I think. He showed that he could think through the answer to a challenging question and then draw it all back into how Batman's qualities and his own qualities would make him a viable fit for the job he was applying for.

In the previous section on common interview questions, I've already listed some common questions which I'd consider to be challenging questions. Questions like "Where do you want to be in five years?", "Can you tell me about a difficult situation you've previously had in a job and how you handled it?", and "What are your weaknesses?" are all commonly asked and challenging interview questions. How you answer those questions may well determine whether you move ahead in the interview process. With this in mind, I strongly suggest that you practice your answers to these questions.

For the fun of it, I've gathered a few other challenging questions for you to consider when you do your mock interviews. Although the chances that you'll be asked these specific questions are very minimal, you should use these questions to hone your thought process in formulating rational and reasonable answers to difficult questions. Although I won't list answers for these questions, as many of them are thought process questions that don't have specific right or wrong answers, I'm hoping that these questions will provide some food for thought as you prepare for your interview.

Here goes:

    1) *"If you were a car, what kind of car would you be and why?"*

    2) *"Why do you think you'd be successful at the job you're applying for?"*

    3) *"Can you explain the employment gap in your resume?"*

    4) "What can you offer us as an employee that other candidates can't?"

    5) *"If you could host a dinner people with four famous people, dead or alive, who would you invite and why?"*

    6) *"How do you manage and prioritize your time?"*

7) *"Can you tell me about a time in the past where you were innovative or 'thought outside the box'?"*

8) *"How to you deal with conflict?"*

9) *"Can you describe an ethical dilemma that you've previously faced and how you handled it?"*

10) *"What has been the biggest failure in your life?"*

11) *"How did you make time for this interview? Where does your boss think you are now?"*

12) *" Have you ever stolen office supplies from a company you've worked for?"*

13) *"Can you tell me about a company policy you're disagreed with and whether and how you expressed you displeasure with that policy?"*

14) *"Can you tell me a reason why people might not like working with you?"*

> 15) *"What would you do if you won $10 million in this week's lottery?"*

And there's one more question I'd like to discuss briefly in this chapter. You may be asked this question or something similar: "What salary do you think you deserve?" This is obviously a key question for both the prospective employer and for the candidate, as if the amount offered by the employer is too low or the amount tendered by the applicant is too high, it can easily be a dealbreaker. As an interview candidate, you will have hopefully researched what salaries are in the job category you're interested in. If you haven't researched, you'll find plenty of available salary information on the internet, including sites like indeed.com, glassdoor.com, payscale.com, and LinkedIn.com. In reviewing the salary ranges for your profession, you should always keep in mind the cost of living in the city where you'll be working. Obviously, the cost of living in New York City or San Francisco will be much higher than it will be for a similar job in Dyersville, Iowa.

When you are asked this salary question, I would highly recommend that you don't give a specific salary. You should first ask the interviewer to confirm the salary range for the job they're offering. For example, if they tell you that the job they are offering is in the $40,000 to $50,000 annual salary range, you'll then at least have a starting point for your negotiations. In most instances, I'd recommend that you request a salary which is higher than the median, unless there's a logical reason why you might be given less than the median. (i.e.—You're less experienced than the other candidates, you're a recent college grad and the other candidates have had previous industry experience, etc.)

Ideally, you won't talk salary on the first interview unless the interviewer is ready to hire you on the spot. If you're applying for a retail position in a department store, you'll probably be discussing salary during the initial interview. If you're applying for an executive position, it's more likely for salary to be discussed in a later interview. In this instance, I would avoid talking salary and compensation package in the initial interview unless the interviewer broaches the subject first.

In reading this section of the book, if there's one thing you can take away from what you've read, I'm hoping that you now understand that the key to answering interview questions, common or challenging, is to prepare and practice. Although the questions you practice answering are likely not to be the same questions you get in the actual interview, it's important that you practice the thought processes you'll need to answer questions you're not familiar with. With preparation and practice, you'll be sure to increase your chance of acing the interview.

Chapter 5—Make a Great First Impression

The first impression you make as you head into your interview can be crucial. I always tell clients that even though it's unlikely that they'll get a job based on their first impression, it's more likely possible that they could lose a job based on their first impression. People who make bad first impressions can lose chances at jobs even before they get a chance to explain what their background, their talents and skills, and why they are the right fit for the job.

With this in mind, I've provided some simple tips on things you can do to make sure you make a great first impression.

Eight Things You Must Do to Make a Killer First Impression.

1) Dress the Part. In an earlier section, I explained the importance of dressing properly for your interview. Again, the main thing you should concentrate on is to make sure that you are properly dressed for the job you're applying for. If you're not exactly sure what to wear, you should remember that it's better to dress up for an interview than it is to dress down.

2) Show Up on Time. As mentioned before, you're certainly going to lose points if you show up late for an interview. We've discussed this previously. If you're going to be late, maybe because of unusually heavy traffic or unusually bad driving conditions, you should certainly call the person you're interviewing with as soon as you realize that you're going to be late. It's not a good idea to keep someone

Job Interview Preparation

waiting; it's worse to keep someone waiting when they don't know you're going to be late. On the other hand, I've not mentioned before that you should try not to arrive too early for an interview. You should not arrive any earlier than 30 minutes ahead of an interview. If you do arrive much earlier than expected, the interviewer may feel rushed or uncomfortable in trying to accommodate you.

3) Be Nice to Everyone. When you're interviewing for a job, it's important that you "put your game face on" as soon as you enter the premises. Be nice to everyone you meet by greeting them with a smile and/or a hello. This includes people you meet in the parking lot, people you meet in the elevator, people you pass in the hall, and certainly the receptionist. Two quick stories: One of my clients was primping on an elevator as she rode up to the third floor for her interview. She looked at herself in her compact mirror, made sure her teeth didn't contain any food particles, made sure her hair looked good. As she did this, she basically ignored the only person who rode up in the elevator with her. You guessed it, the person who rode up in the elevator with her was the person who she was interviewing with. When my client discovered this, she was frantic in trying to remember what she had done in front of the person she rode the elevator with and she was embarrassed to think that she hadn't at least greeted the other person riding in the elevator. Another of my clients carried on a conversation with the receptionist in the lobby at the company where he was interviewing. The receptionist wasn't very busy. It seems that her primary responsibility

was to answer the phones and the phones weren't ringing, so the receptionist was open to a chat. After my client was hired, he found out that the interviewer's best friend was the receptionist and the interviewer routinely solicited the receptionist's first impression of the people who interviewed there. Thanks to his pleasant conversation with the receptionist, my client got some bonus points even before his official interview began. So, bottom line is, when you go to an interview, it's important for you to get into the mindset of being friendly to everyone you meet. You never know when the impressions you make will impact your chances of getting a job.

4) Put Your Phone Away. It's obvious that you'll want to turn your phone off during the interview itself. But I suggest that you put it away from the time you enter the lobby. I'll note below the importance of being engaged during an interview. You can't be engaged in an interview if you're spending time on your phone. Back in the days in which I was interviewing for jobs, I always found the time I spent in the lobby waiting for the interview to be educational. It was interesting to see how the receptionist greeted other visitors and co-workers. It was also interesting to see how the company's workers interacted with each other. In one of my interviews, in the 20 minutes I spent in the lobby, I noticed that the body language and the interactions of the people who worked at that company were unusually negative. As a result, even before I went into the interview, I was questioning whether I wanted to work there. Sure enough, the human resources person was out of the same negative mold and I left the building knowing that I would

not accept the offer I received. I was glad that I had put my phone away and was cognizant of what the workplace environment was.

5) Be Engaged, Be Interested. In interviewing for any job, it's important that you show your interest or enthusiasm. I always tell clients to make sure they are engaged from the time they enter the door of the office or the door of the building in which they are interviewing. Pay attention to the things that are visible in the lobby and in the office of the person you're interviewing with. An average interview might last 45 minutes. Those 45 minutes could be a major factor in determining your future. With this in mind, any interview you have deserves your undivided attention and your undeterred enthusiasm.

6) Be Confident. It's important that you look confident going into an interview. Pay attention to your body language, your posture, and your demeanor. When you meet someone, make sure to introduce yourself, offer a firm handshake, and make eye contact. I've noted before that whenever I've been the interviewer, I've docked applicants who have a flimsy handshake or failed to look me in the eye when they're introduced to me.

7) Make Sure You Know Who You're Talking To. This seems so obvious, but I've had clients who've made the grave error of calling their interviewer by the wrong name throughout the interview. I had a client who addressed

Janel as Jolene throughout the interview and I'm sure she lost some serious points for doing so. Make sure you have the interviewer's name going into the interview. It's desirable to use the name of the interviewer(s) throughout the interview, but you have to make sure you're using the right name.

8) Find Common Ground, Make a Connection. With any interview, it's important for you to make a connection or find common ground with the people you're interviewing with. Again, you'll probably be competing against other candidates in getting the job, and you'll want to separate yourself from those other candidates by possibly making a connection with the person who was interviewing you. From the time you enter the building, or the conference room or office where the interview is being conducted, you should observe your surroundings to see if you can find anything that will help you to make a connection with the interviewer. Are there company newsletters in the lobby for guests to read, a company trophy case or history case? What personal belongings do you spot in the office of your interviewer? Family photos, softball or bowling trophies, college diploma, etc. Can you use any of these things to find common ground? Many years ago, I was trying to get the business of a man who would later become a big client for my company. Upon meeting him for the first time in his office, I noted that he had a baseball trophy on one of the shelves in his office and also he had a framed version of a Minnesota Twins baseball pennant and World Series tickets hanging on his wall. I surmised immediately that this man was a baseball fan and, as an avid baseball fan

myself, I started our conversation off by asking him if he was a baseball fan. Sure enough, he was, and we found common ground immediately. To this day, I swear that one of the reasons I was able to secure his business was because we had a common love of baseball. Of course, none of this would have mattered if my company hadn't been a good fit for his business, but our mutual love of baseball allowed me to separate myself from other candidates immediately. I've had clients that have been able to do the same thing with mutual alma maters, comparing kids ("Are these your sons? I have three sons…."),etc. If you can find common ground or make a connection with your interviewer, you're likely to enhance your chances of landing the job.

How to Instantly Stand Out Among Other Candidates.

As I've noted before, job interviews are a competition of sorts. There are multiple candidates for almost all job openings and if you're going to get the job you're probably going to have to stand out from your competition. If you don't, you're likely to be forgotten quickly.

When my clients ask me how they can stand out in an interview, I have a number of suggestions on how to do so:

I've previously noted how important it is for you to do your homework heading into an interview. One of the surest ways to stand out in an interview is to know more about the company than anyone else. Most interviews offer plenty of opportunities to show that they've done their research and to show how much they know about the company. Obviously, the questions you ask during an interview can also show that you've researched the company thoroughly. If you don't show the interviewer that you know anything about the company you're

Job Interview Preparation

interviewing with, they're likely to think that you're not very interested in the job.

Another way to stand out in an interview is to simply be yourself. I encourage clients to be themselves during an interview, if only because so many people are not good at pretending to be someone we are not. We're not play actors and if you're trying to be someone else during the interview, most interviewers will be able to detect that. Another reason I encourage clients to be themselves is because if they actually land the job, the employer is probably going to find out quickly who the employee really is anyway. So, as strange as it sounds, you can stand out in an interview by being yourself.

And here's an important way for you to stand out. Treat your interviews like conversations. Interviewing is a two-way street. You're not going to make a good impression if you treat the interview like a college exam or a police interrogation, with the interviewer asking all the questions and you dutifully providing all the answers. It's important that you try to turn the interview into a conversation. You can do this by asking related questions throughout the interview process. Again, as I've mentioned many times before, if you're going to turn the interview into a conversation instead of an interrogation, you're going to have to be totally engaged in what's being said throughout the interview. Listen intently and then ask questions or add comments as you see fit. A good way to do this is to end your answer with a related question. For example, if you're asked why you think you're a good fit for the job you're interviewing for, you might say, "From everything I've read or heard about this company, it is a company that cares deeply about its customers. I'm the same way. I derive a great deal of satisfaction in knowing that my customers value the products and services I sell. This company seems to do a better job of that than its competitors. Am I right in thinking that and can you

Job Interview Preparation

share why you think that is?" Note that the interviewee has answered the question and then followed it up with a related question of their own, a question which is not a yes or no question, one that will hopefully help turn the interview into more of a conversation than an interrogation or exam.

Another way to stand out in an interview will be to provide an additional one-sheet summary, other than your resume and your cover letter, explaining why you're a good fit for the specific job you're applying for. I've had some clients who will present this summary during the interview and other clients who will send this summary after an interview. Some of my clients swear by this technique, regardless of whether it's presented during or after the interview. I've also had clients who have submitted 30-, 60-, or 90-day plans on what they would hope to accomplish in their first days of working for the company. These plans are almost always presented in the days immediately following the interview (obviously before the company has made a hiring decision). In doing something additional to just the standard resume and cover letter, you'll be able to reiterate your sincere interest in the job.

If the interviewer asks you for examples of how you've been successful in your previous jobs, I'll remind you again to use numbers whenever possible to document your success. i.e.—"I was responsible for increasing sales in the Northeast Region by 135% in the first two years I had that region." Or another example: "As a franchise development director, we went from 45 franchised print shops to 87 franchised print shops within a year. The company goal when I arrived there was to open 20 locations per year and my team and I were able to exceed that by 22 locations." Bottom line is that numbers work in illustrating success and achievement. With numbers, you can turn an intangible statement into a tangible one.

And, finally, another way for you to stand out after an interview is the send a handwritten thank you/enjoyed meeting you note. Yes, I said handwritten, not typed. Handwritten is so much more personal than a typed note. If the company is very close to you, you might even hand-deliver it. If not, you can send it via the US Post Office or a delivery service, but send it immediately, within 24 hours. And, obviously make sure your spelling, grammar, and punctuation are correct.

Confident Body Language that Puts You Ahead of the Game.

So, you think you've done everything possible to make a great first impression. You're impeccably dressed, you polished your shoes, got a haircut, and manicured your nails. Yet, if you don't pay attention to the signals your body is sending, your body can work against you and impair the image you're trying to convey with your appearance. Body language is important. We all know people who can capture a room when they walk into it. In just a matter of seconds, people will form perceptions on a person based on their body language. So, all the time and money you spent for the new suit, the haircut, and even the new leather portfolio can all get blown to bits in just a moment.

One of the key elements of body language is proper posture. If you want to display an air of confidence, it's important that you "walk tall"…stand straight, chin up, eyes up. Certainly, no slumping or slouching. Nothing worse than slinking into a room.

I've already mentioned the importance of a firm handshake when being introduced to someone. Yes, there's an art to doing something as simple as a handshake. When you're introduced to your interviewer, put away your floppy fish handshake and replace it with your "big boy" handshake. Male or female, you should offer a firm, genuine handshake. That being said, don't shake hands so firmly that you're going to crush the other person's hand. Always stand, and never sit, when you are shaking hands. Don't pull the other person toward you with your handshake…it's not an arm wrestling match. And avoid sweaty hands. And beware that there are some people who do not want to shake hands. Most of us know some people who are germophobes who try to avoid physical contact whenever possible. If you run into an interviewer who is a germophobe, don't take it personally.

At the same time you're shaking hands with someone, you need to make eye contact with them. And continue to do that as much as possible throughout the interview. In making eye contact with someone, you'll exude a sense of confidence, genuineness, and sincerity. Remember that one of your goals for the interview will be to create a bond or a connection with your interviewer. Eye contact can help you do that. If you're looking down at the floor or over at the wall when you're shaking hands with your interviewer, you may well give them the idea that you're insecure.

Besides your posture and your eyes, pay attention to what you're doing with your arms and legs throughout the interview. Don't cross your legs, when you're standing or sitting. Don't place your hands on your hips when you're standing. Don't lean toward one side. Don't cross your arms over your chest at any time. Body language experts will tell you that's a defensive position that doesn't play well with the person you're meeting with.

And pay attention to what you're doing with your hands throughout the interview. If you're someone who does a lot of hand gesturing, don't do any pointing, as that can come across as threatening. Open palm/open hand gestures are considered OK. If you are a bit of a fidgeter, try not to tap your fingers or your toes during the interview.

And don't play with your hair, repeatedly click your pen, jiggle the coins in your pockets, etc. Some of those quirks or bad habits are likely to make a bad impression with the people you meet in your interview.

And finally, smile whenever it is appropriate. And don't be afraid to show those pearly whites, unless you have bad teeth. I can speak from personal experience in regards to facial expressions. People have told me before that I have a stern face. Since that look tends to make me look grumpy or unapproachable, whenever I meet someone in person now, I make sure to make an extra effort to offer a big smile that will make me more welcoming and more approachable.

So, in recapping this chapter, let me again emphasize the importance of making a good first impression in an interview. Although you probably won't be able to land the job with the good first impression you make, you could lose a chance at a job with a bad first impression. That's why you should not ignore the visual impression you are making with the interview. By paying attention to a few minor details, you'll be assured that you've not lost the job before the interview actually starts.

Job Interview Preparation

Chapter 6—Pass with Flying Colors

As you interview for jobs, you'll have an advantage toward getting the job of your dreams if you have an understanding of what interviewers want to hear. Along the same lines, you'll benefit from knowing some things you should never say in an interview. And then, you'll also want to convey to the interviewer that you have the soft skills which will ensure your standing as a valuable employee and place you above the other candidates for the same job. (For those of you who aren't familiar with soft skills, I'll explain that in more detail later in this chapter.)

11 Things Your Prospective Employer Wants to Hear.

When you interview for a job, you'll likely be asked a lot of questions. Some job candidates make the mistake of not understanding why the interviewer is asking the questions they're asking. If you have a feel for why your interviewer is asking the questions they're asking, you'll find it much easier to determine the things they want to hear from you. Here are some things that interviewers love to hear from candidates, in no particular order.

1) "I'm self-motivated. If you give me a project, I can take it from start to finish...and I can get it done in time. You won't have to micromanage me. I can work with minimal supervision."

Job Interview Preparation

2) *"I take direction well. You won't have to tell me the same thing multiple times. If you tell me what to do once, you won't have to tell me again."*

3) *"I am a good communicator. I'll keep you and my co-workers updated on any projects I'm working on."*

4) *"I work and play well with others. I'm a team player, not a lone wolf."*

5) *"I can lead or I can follow. I do both well."*

6) *"I'm teachable. I'm quick to admit that I don't know everything and I'm willing and anxious to learn from others."*

7) *"I have the skills to do the job."* (Reiterate your skills here.)

8) *"I'm a good fit for this job and I'm a good fit for this company."* (Detail why you're a good fit here.)

9) *"I'm loyal. I'll be loyal to my supervisor and loyal to the company."*

10) *"My goals and objectives coincide with the mission and purpose of this company."*

11) *"I want to say again that I would love the opportunity to work here."* (Presuming that you're still excited about the job as the interview nears its conclusion, you should reiterate your interest and enthusiasm toward the job before you leave the interview. If you want the job, you should make sure they know that you want the job.)

Eight Things You Won't Want to Say in a Job Interview.

Just as there are some things you should definitely try to mention in your interview, there are things that you should not say in an interview. I've listed some common mistakes people make in interviews below. Hopefully, these mistakes will give you an idea of what not to say during an interview.

1) *"So, what do you do here?"* Someone hasn't done their homework.

2) *"I know I don't have much experience, but…"* No need to point out your shortcomings and to display a lack of confidence at the same time. If the interviewer has your resume or application, they'll already know that you are short on experience.

3) *"I didn't get along with my boss"* or *"I didn't like the last company I worked for."* Trashing past employers is not going to be helpful.

4) *"How much vacation time do I get?"* This is better discussed in a subsequent interview when you are discussing salary or the compensation package.

5) *"I'd like to start my own business as soon as possible."* Why should someone hire you when you're looking to leave as soon as possible.

6) *"I'll do whatever you want me to do."* Sounds way too desperate.

7) *"How soon do you promote employees."* Again, this comes across as desperate and will probably make the interviewer think that you can't wait to get past the position they're hiring for.

8) *"No, I don't have any questions."* I've discussed this previously. If the interviewer asks if you have any questions, don't pass up the opportunity to ask relevant questions. Not only can you use the questions to gain any additional information you're looking for, you'll be able to convey your interest in the position to the interviewer.

10 Soft Skills and How to Demonstrate Them.

When we talk about demonstrating soft skills, I realize that some of you may not know what soft skills are. With this in mind, let me first tell you what soft skills are. Soft skills are personal attributes,

Job Interview Preparation

personality traits, social cues, or communication abilities. Soft skills are generally a lot less tangible qualities than hard skills. Hard skills are specific job skills or certifications. Examples of hard skills are high school diplomas, college or trade school degrees, professional licenses or certifications, training program completions, on-the-job training, job experience, etc. Hard skills are specific and tangible job skills or proof of job skills. Soft skills are less tangible qualities that are normally not graded by degrees, certificates, or licenses.

When a company is evaluating your resume, they'll generally look first at the hard skills you've listed on your resume. They want to make sure that your hard skills comply with their requirements and also they'll probably want to compare your hard skills with those of the other candidates. For example, if they're looking for an accounting manager, they're generally going to be looking for someone who has an accounting degree and possibly someone who has passed the CPA Board Exam. Those are tangible, hard skills. If you don't have those hard skills, you're likely to be eliminated from the competition.

After these prospective employers have determined your hard skills, they'll then move to your soft skills. If you've "passed" the hard skill requirements, it's likely that whether or not you get the job will be determined by your soft skills. Below I've listed some of the most common soft skills that employers are looking for. As you know, most resumes and cover letters have limited space. Although I encourage you to incorporate your soft skills into your resumes and cover letters, I am aware that there's rarely enough room for you to list all of your soft skills. As a result, it's very important that you mention that you have these skills in your interview. In listing soft skills on your resume, I suggest that you label them as "Transferable Skills", as those are qualities that can usually be transferred to just about any job you're applying for.

For the most part, soft skills are acquired over a period of time instead of in classes or training sessions. Whereas someone can get a journalism major by taking college journalism classes, people generally don't get soft skills such as communication skills, creative skills, or problem-solving skills by taking classes. These soft skills are normally acquired by "learning through experience", or the "school of hard knocks" as some would say.

Soft skills are often considered invaluable by employers, as they are transferable skills that can be used in just about any job. Customer service jobs or jobs in which employees come into direct contact with customers are particularly conducive to soft skills.

In determining which soft skills you want to promote, you should read the posting for that position and you note any soft skills which are mentioned in that posting. These are skills that you should be sure to work into your resume, your cover letter, and your interview, presuming you have the skills they are describing.

For example, if the job posting mentions that the company is looking for someone to become part of their team or the key words in the posting include words such as "team", "teamwork", or "works with others", you'll then know that the company is looking for someone who has this skill. Almost all job postings mention at least a couple of soft skills that the employer is looking for.

Here are some common soft skills which companies are looking for in the people they hire:

    1) Motivated or self-motivated.
    2) Hard worker or strong work ethic.
    3) Adaptability.
    4) Team player, able to work well with others.

5) Communicator.
6) Creative thinker, think outside the box, critical thinking.
7) Decision making.
8) Able to resolve conflicts or solve problems.
9) Time management, ability to prioritize.
10) Positivity, enthusiasm.

Again, prior to your interview, you should review the soft skills which are mentioned in the job posting and take an inventory of your own soft skills to see which skills correspond to those that the prospective employer is looking for. Then, you should develop a plan on how you can let the interviewer know you have these skills. For example, if the posting mentions that the employer is looking for a hard worker and you are indeed a hard worker, you'll need to figure out how to drop this into your interview. It won't matter whether you drop this information into the interview directly or indirectly, but you definitely need to let the interview know that you are a hard worker.

If you can provide specific examples to show that you are a hard worker, that's even better. For example, a client of mine was interviewing for a public relations job in which the primary responsibility included events planning. The posting for this job had mentioned that the company was looking to hire someone that was willing to work hard if necessary to complete a project. So, during her interview, my client mentioned that she was a hard worker and she was willing to work whatever hours were necessary to meet the goals of the department or to complete projects on time. She gave the specific example of how she had coordinated a milk carton boat race in one of her previous jobs. (Yes, boats made of milk cartons.) Her company had been the sole sponsor of this event and her supervisor and the management team had underestimated the amount of time it would take to put this even together. As a result, my client and her two team members had to work 12-hour days, 7 days a week in the two weeks prior to the event to make sure that it went off as planned. As a result of the work of her and her team members, the event went off flawlessly and she received plenty of thank you's from company executives who recognized her hard work and a special thank you from the supervisor who had underestimated the amount of time it would take to plan the event.

As you can see, my client not only mentioned that she was a hard worker, she also told a story that showed that she was a hard worker, willing to do whatever was necessary to make the event a success.

I'll give you another example. Another company looking for a customer service representative mentioned that they were looking for candidates who were problem solvers. One of my clients was applying for this job with a promotional products company, a company that provides custom-imprinted items such as t-shirts, pens, tote bags, etc. for corporate customers. My client had previous experience with a promotional products company and he told this story when asked to describe a problem situation in a previous job and how she handled it. A customer had ordered daily calendar refills every year for many years. One year, the customer was delayed in placing their order and by the time my client went to order these calendar refills for her customer, the factory was sold out of them and they were not going to be getting more of these refills, as they were made in Malaysia and the delivery time to receive additional refill pads was going to be well into March or April of the upcoming year. Instead of just dropping this problem back into her customer's lap, my client worked immediately to find another factory that had similar, but not identical, refills that would work. She had to do about three hours of research and make about a dozen phone calls to come up with a solution to the problem, but she did. She then contacted her customer to make them aware of the initial problem and, at the same time, explain that she had found a solution. She immediately offered to send the customer a photo of the alternate calendar refill pads and the customer found them to be acceptable. All of this for a customer who was placing a small order of about $150.

This story certainly showed my client's ability to attack a problem and solve it, despite the small size of the order. It shows that she was able to go "above and beyond" to solve a problem on behalf of her customer.

If you can find a way to effectively communicate your soft skills to your interviewer, you'll give yourself a much better chance to land the job.

Chapter 7—Finishing Touches

With this chapter, I'm going to tell you how to put the finishing touches on what will hopefully be a successful interview. I'll give you some questions you can ask the interviewer, I'll tell you how to broach the salary and compensation package discussion, and I'll tell you what to do when and if a question catches you off-guard. And we'll also discuss if and when it's OK to lie or embellish during an interview.

11 Great Questions to Ask the Hiring Manager.

As we've discussed before, the more you can turn your interview into a conversation instead of an interrogation or an exam, the more successful you'll be. Remember, interviews are two-way streets. The interviewer should not be the only person gathering information. You should also be asking the questions you'll need to know about the job you're applying for.

Toward the end of almost every interview, the interviewer or hiring manager is likely to ask you if you have any questions. As we've discussed before, the worst possible way to answer this question is to say that you don't have any questions. If you do this, the interviewer is likely to think that you're either unprepared or you're disinterested.

You should view this question from the interviewer as an opportunity to gather any additional information you're looking for and also to emphasize again the qualities, skills, experience, and reason why you're a good fit for the job.

Again, I strongly suggest that you prepare some questions in advance, at least a half-dozen. And then, as the interview winds down and you get asked if you have any questions, you should select two or three questions to ask of the interviewer. As the interviewer is likely to answer some of the questions you had prior to the interview, make sure you don't ask questions requesting information for subjects that have already been covered. If you do that, the interviewer will know for sure that you weren't paying attention to what he or she said during the interview. On the other hand, as you and the interviewer talk during the interview, you're likely to come up with some additional questions that are more pertinent than the questions you had originally intended to ask.

Below are some of the types of questions you might ask of the interviewer during this part of the conversation. A few quick things before we get into these sample questions: When you ask questions of the interviewer, try not to ask them questions that have yes or no answers. Ask them questions that they can expound upon. And, on the other hand, don't ask questions which are going to stump them or which they're not going to know the answers to. For example, if you're interviewing with the human resources person for an advertising position, you shouldn't be asking them technical questions about advertising methods or advertising philosophies. Those questions will be better asked of the ad director who you are likely to meet in a subsequent interview. And finally, although I'll cover this in more detail later, the first question out of your mouth should not be "What's the salary?" In my previous experiences as an interviewer, I had an applicant ask me this question less than two minutes into the interview. I immediately ruled him out as a candidate and cut what was supposed to be a 45-minute interview to a 20-minute interview. I also had another candidate ask, soon after he sat down, "So, what do you all do here?". I immediately knew that he hadn't done any research, other than maybe how to drive to the interview, and I ruled him out immediately.

Job Interview Preparation

Here are some questions you might ask in your interviewer when you get the opportunity to do so:

1) *"Can you tell me a bit about the company culture or what's it's like to work here?"* This is something you'll definitely want to find out before you accept the position.

2) *"What are the next steps in the interview process?"*. *"When are you looking to have someone on board for this position?"* And if you're meeting with a human resources person or a hiring manager, you should definitely find out who you'll be reporting to and if you'll be able to meet that person during the interview process.

3) *"Will this job offer an eventual opportunity for advancement?"* *"Can you tell me if any of the people who previously held this position advanced in the company or in their career path?"*

4) *"Is this a new position or are you looking to fill a position that someone previously filled? And, if you don't mind me asking, what did the person who previously filled this position go on to do?"* Or, you can simply ask, *"Why is this job open or available?"*

5) *"Does this job require a lot of travel?"* *"Is there any chance that I'd be relocated in this position?"*

Job Interview Preparation

6) *"What are the company's plans for growth and development? "What are the department's plans?"*

7) *"What's the best part of working for this company?" "What's the most challenging part?"* Again, another question that might help you gain some additional insight regarding the company culture.

8) *"Is there anything I can clarify for you regarding my qualifications?"* This question might help you identify if the interviewer has any concerns and, if so, you'll then be able to address those concerns.

9) In the unlikely scenario that the interviewer hasn't explained the responsibilities of the job, you should ask. Along the same lines, you might ask, *"Can you give me an idea of what a typical day in this position might look like?"*

10) *"What's an average work week look like? Do most employees put in a lot of extra hours?"*

11) And finally, *"What's next?"* or *"When might I expect to hear from you?"*, *"When would you like me to contact you?"* or *"Is it OK if I follow up in a couple of days?"* Don't leave the interview without finding out what the next step is. If you leave without getting this information, you'll have to spend a lot of time guessing whether you're still in the running for the job or not.

An Essential Guide to Salary Negotiations.

Depending on the job you apply for, you may have the opportunity to negotiate salary. Of course, there are some jobs in which the salary level is already set. My neighbor's son recently interviewed for a job as a seasonal salesperson in a retail chain. It's obvious that a position in a structured corporate environment like this is going to have pre-determined salary structures and you're not going to be able to negotiate your salary as an entry level employee. These are jobs that are what I call single interview jobs, in which only one interview is required before an applicant will be extended an offer or eliminated from the competition.

On the other hand, most multiple interview situations allow for some salary negotiations. Now, while we can all claim that money should never be the main factor in which to take a job, you also have to remember that the amount you're paid may well have an effect on how you perceive the job. If you're not happy with the salary you're getting or you feel that your salary doesn't properly reflect the talents and abilities you bring to the company, you may find that your salary (or lack of it) makes you discouraged, resentful, or even angry. If you're disappointed in the salary you're making, you may even find that your disappointment leads to poor performance.

In my previous work life, I worked for a company that was notorious for underpaying its employees. It was a great place to work…except for the salaries they paid their employees. As a result of this reputation, employees who worked for this company were the frequent targets of headhunters or corporate recruiters who were looking to place people in different jobs. At that time, I was a rising young executive inside the company and I held a position that carried a lot of responsibility. I was a hard worker and very good at what I did; even my supervisors said so. In this position, I frequently received calls from headhunters offering me interviews for similar positions that paid much higher salaries. As a 26-year-old, I wasn't looking to leave a company I liked working for, but I was fully aware that a higher salary might help me get out of the position of living check-to-check. I was hoping to pay off my college loans and then purchase a modest house. Some of the interview opportunities the headhunters described included salaries that were more than double what I was making and, generally, those jobs carried a lot less responsibility than the job I had. So, it was deflating to know that I wasn't paid fairly. I resisted the weekly requests for interviews for quite a while, but eventually my salary level tainted my perception of the job I had. I eventually started to accept some of the interview invitations and eventually accepted a job that offered almost three times what I had been making.

The moral of the story is that regardless of how unimportant salary might seem, you'll still have bills to pay and you'll still want to make sure you're paid fairly. If you're not paid fairly, you'll probably find that your lack of salary will likely impact your attitude and possibly affect your performance.

Hopefully, you'll have an idea going into the interview what the "market rates" are for the job you're interested in. If you're not sure, you can use various internet sites to obtain salary information. Sites such as indeed.com, glassdoor.com, and LinkedIn all offer industry salary information that you can use as a guideline.

It's important to note that salary is generally discussed near the end of an interview situation. In a multiple interview situation, you might first have a phone interview and/or a video interview before you actually interview with someone face to face. In these instances, you'll find that salary is rarely discussed in the initial interviews. That being said, you should never wait until the very end of an interview to discuss salary or the compensation package. Salary should not be an afterthought and, if you wait too long to discuss salary, you'll lose some of the leverage you might have in negotiating it.

Normally the interviewer will be first to broach the topic, but if they are not doing that and it seems like it's time to discuss salary, you can segue into this discussion by asking something like, "Would now be a good time to talk salary?"

Ideally, you'll be able to get the interviewer to give you a salary range before you have to give up too much information regarding your salary requirements. Some interviewers are likely to ask you what your salary is in your current position. If you're asked this question, I encourage you to be careful not to impart too much information. If you blurt out your current salary, you'll almost certainly be restricting the salary you would be offered in the new job. For example, if you're making an annual salary of $40,000 and you tell the interviewer that, you're likely not to get a salary that exceeds your existing salary by more than 10%. Research shows that many employers are reluctant to increase salaries of new employees substantially if they know the new employee's current salary level and they feel that an increase of around 10% is enough to get someone to leave another job.

So, ideally, you will ask the prospective employer if they have a salary range in mind for the job. If they continue to press you for your current salary, you might respond by saying, "What I make in my current position really isn't relevant, as this would be a different job with a different company and different responsibilities. I'm just looking for a job that will pay me fairly based on my talents and abilities." And then you might add the question, "Can you tell me what kind of budget range you have for this position?"

It should be noted that I would never recommend that you lie about your current salary. Although some people do that, and do it successfully, you should know that if you get caught in a lie, you'll blow your chance to get the job immediately. Also remember that you might have filled out an application on which you were asked to list your current salary. In filling out this portion of an application, I tell my clients to list their desired salary on this line of the application. I.e.—(Desired salary range is $50,000/year.)

So, again, try not to volunteer your current salary information too quickly (unless you're already paid about market rate. In disclosing your salary, you're likely to lose some of your leverage in negotiating a higher salary.

What to Do When You Get a Question that Throws You Off-Guard.

Regardless of how long or how hard you prepare for an interview, you're likely to get one or two questions that will throw you off-guard. Don't let these questions fluster you or "throw you for a loop". I have some simple tips which will allow you more time to gather your thoughts.

You can buy more time to develop your answer by simply acknowledging the question. Here are some sample acknowledgments:

--*"Oh, that's a good question."*

--*"Oh, I've never been asked that before."*

-- "Let me think about that for a moment."

--If you think you can come up with a good answer to the question, you might say, "I'm glad you asked that."

Another way to buy more time is to simply rephrase or repeat the question. "If I were a tree, what kind of tree would I be and why?" or "So, what kind of tree would I be?"

And, if you don't totally understand the question, you can ask the interviewer to clarify the question. "I want to make sure I understand the question. Can I ask you to expand on that or to clarify?"

And, finally, if the question asked of you is a multi-layered question, feel free to jot down some notes as to how you might answer. But if you're taking notes, make sure that you take them quickly. You won't want to hold up the interview while you take notes.

Is It OK to Lie?; When Is It OK to Lie in an Interview?

It's no secret that some people lie in interviews. Maybe it's the pressure of getting that job that you really want. Maybe it's the idea, sometimes true, that lying, embellishing, or omitting certain information from an interview will help you get the job.

Although I strongly discourage you from lying to your prospective employer, there might be things you can embellish or omit certain information in an interview. I'll give you some examples, in no particular order:

Job Interview Preparation

1) Salary. This is the number one thing that people lie about in their interviews. I recommend against this, as it could come back to bite you later, especially if the human resources department from your new company checks your references and the question of your salary comes up. Instead of making up a salary that is higher than you receive in your current position, you might put a price tag on your current compensation package, including salary, vacation time, benefits, etc. i.e.—"I have a compensation and benefits package that I would value near $150,000."

2) Your talents and abilities. Some people will lie about what they can do. For example, when asked if they are familiar with a particular software program, they might indicate that they are familiar with it when they don't know how to use this. If this is something you can take a crash course on and learn between the interview and your start date, you could probably get away with it. But if you're not familiar with the program and can't learn it quickly, you're going to be in trouble when you are actually on the job and your employer expects you to know how to use the program. You'll be better off being honest and telling the interviewer that you are not familiar with the program, but that you are a fast and willing learner and willing to learn that skill quickly. I knew a graphic designer who lied about the graphic programs he was familiar with. He was hired for the job. But two days into the job, his employer figured out that the new employee wasn't familiar with the graphics programs he said he was, and that graphic artist was terminated less than a week into his new job.

3) How you feel about your current boss or co-workers. This is an area in which you can do some harm to yourself. If you had major conflicts with current or past bosses or co-workers, you will not benefit from trashing them in your interview. No, you certainly don't have to sing their praises, however you won't accomplish anything by trashing them either.

4) Your greatest weaknesses. If a prospective employer inquires about what your greatest weaknesses are, it's probably OK for you to highlight a weakness other than your greatest weakness. Instead of admitting a weakness that can't be corrected easily, you should select a weakness that you can or maybe have already improved upon. i.e.— "I previously took on more projects than I could handle, without delegating. I realized that shortcoming and have since worked to utilize my team much better. Although, I'm still working on this, I now feel like I've improved to the level where it's no longer a problem."

5) Who you know. It's OK to drop names during an interview, but make sure that you at least know the person you say you know, as this is yet another thing that can come back to bite you if you lie.

6) Your interests. If you're asked what your main interests are outside of work, it's probably OK to select lesser interests that make you look better to a prospective employer. Although, beware. I knew a young man who

professed that he loved to golf, when he saw golf trophies in the interviewer's office. He didn't golf at all and soon after he was hired, the interviewer kept asking him if he wanted to join in a round of golf. The young man continued to decline, but he told me that the interviewer who was now his co-worker eventually figured out that the young man was not a golfer and, although the young man wasn't fired, he was embarrassed by the situation.

7) Fired or quit. If you were fired or laid off from your past position, be honest about it, but don't dwell on it. Focus on the positive and tell your employer that you're ready for new challenges and opportunities.

8) Places you've worked. If you've had places you've worked at for short periods of time or places where you had a bad experience, it's OK for you to leave that off your resume or out of the interview conversation, as long as you can explain any employment gaps in your resume.

Again, no one can tell you whether you should lie, embellish, or omit information during your interview. You'll have to determine this based on your ethics and the principles you live by. However, if you do lie or embellish, I strongly suggest that you examine the possible consequences of doing so.

Chapter 8—The Future is Waiting

Your interview is over. You either got the job or you didn't, or you'll have to wait for the prospective employer to make a decision. Either way, there are some things you should do to follow up on your interview.

What to do after the job interview.

Before you hang up the phone, sign off from a video call, or leave the interview, it's extremely important for you to ask the interviewer when to follow up (presuming they didn't announce a decision before the interview ended). If you interviewed with multiple people, find out who you should follow up with and how the interviewer would prefer that you follow up. (Do they want you to call, do they want you to email them?, etc.)

After you've cleared your head, I suggest that you sit down and write or type some notes from the interview. As days pass after an interview, you're likely to forget some of the things that were discussed during the interview and you'll probably find it beneficial to have some notes which you can refer back to, if necessary.

After you've done that, you should plan to send a thank you note to each person you interviewed with. If you had a phone interview or a video interview, an emailed thank you note is appropriate. If you've had a face-to-face interview, I would recommend that you send an email thank you that same day and then a handwritten snail mail thank you that day or the following day. If you are emailing thank you notes to multiple people, write a personal and different note to each person

Job Interview Preparation

you interviewed with. Preferably not the same note copied. An emailed note will afford you the opportunity to reiterate your interest in the job and emphasize again why you are the right fit for the job. The snail mail note should be much shorter, probably on a thank you card of some kind. With both note forms, I recommend that you always thank the interviewers for their time, tell them that you enjoyed learning more about the position and the company, and again express your interest and enthusiasm for the job they are offering.

In sending thank you notes, you should note that you're probably not going to get a job based on a thank you note, but if you don't send a note, you could lose the job. Thank you notes offer applicants the chance to stay "top of mind" with interviewers and if you don't send a thank you not or follow up as agreed upon, the interviewer may well think that you're not interested in the job.

If you are working with a corporate recruiter or a headhunter in your job search, ask your recruiter to follow up with a phone call to the hiring manager. They should be able to find out how you did in the interview. Even if you're working with a recruiter, the thank you notes need to come from you and not the recruiter. The interviewer needs to understand that you're interested in the job, not just that the recruiter is interested in placing you. And, if you're using a recruiter, I suggest that you personally follow up with the interviewer instead of leaving the task solely to the recruiter.

Hopefully, you've made note of when the interviewer asked you to follow up with them. A couple of notes regarding these follow-ups. Follow up when the interview told you to follow up. Not sooner, not later. You may have to walk a fine line between seeming interested in the job and seeming desperate or becoming a nuisance. When following up, ask them for an update on where they are in the hiring process and with each call or email ask them when you should contact them again to get an updated status. And, if it feels appropriate, you might ask them how you are stacking up against the other candidates they've interviewed. If you can get an answer on this, you'll have a better inkling as to what your chances are to get the job.

And while you are waiting to hear on one job, don't let that stop you from searching for other jobs. Depending on what positions you're interviewing for, getting a job can sometimes be a numbers game and there's no harm in interviewing for multiple jobs at the same time. If you get an offer on one job while you're waiting to hear on another job that you would prefer more, you'll then have a decision to make, but that will be a nice problem to have.

You Got the Job! Now what?

Bingo! You got the job! That great news should sets in motion the things you'll need to do to transition from you old job to your new job.

Upon receiving a job offer, you should confirm the offer with a letter of acceptance. In the letter, you should confirm the agreed-upon start date, salary, and entire compensation package (if the employer hasn't already confirmed these things in writing with their offer). Make a copy of your letter of acceptance for future reference if questions should arise later.

Then you will need to tell your current boss that you have accepted a position with another company. You can do this verbally or with a formal letter of resignation. When you are submitting a letter of resignation, you should also copy the human resources person in your company. If you're initially informing your boss of your new job in writing, you should then offer to meet with him or her at their convenience to establish a transition plan. You should know that there are some companies who will not allow you to continue to work there after you've submitted a letter of resignation. Don't take this personally, as some companies have that policy and it shouldn't be taken personally. A client of mine hosts a radio talk show. When he got a job at another station three years ago, station management told him that he would not be allowed on air anymore. He'd worked there for seven years and he took that as a personal affront, disappointed that he would not be allowed to say goodbye to all the people who had loyally listened to his radio show over the years. I told him not to take that personally, as it was simply company policy. (The station was owned by a media conglomerate that had previously been burned by allowing a departing employee to continue on the air waves after that employee had tendered his resignation. The employee proceeded to "trash" the station with lots of negative comments during his final radio show. Thus, there was a reason for the company policy.)

In any letter of resignation or any of your actions following your resignation, I strongly suggest that you take the high road and remain gracious throughout the process, even if you had things about working there that you didn't like. It's never good to burn bridges in leaving a job. That might make you feel better, but it will also show a lack of respect for the people who continue to work there and you never know if you'll need something from one of those people in the future. Any letter of resignation should note that you were happy for the opportunity to work there and that you wish them success in the future (even if you might not).

In meeting with your soon-to-be former boss or supervisor, it will be good if you can agree on a transition plan. Will your supervisor want you to train someone else for the position you're leaving? Will he want you to provide detailed instructions for your replacement? I've had many clients who have been quick to offer their new contact information to their former supervisor, telling them that they are welcome to call any time they have questions regarding the position they left. If you don't think that your previous employer will become a nuisance with lots of phone calls, this is probably OK. However, if you're going to do this, you should be aware that it is possible that your new employer may frown upon this practice and you might want to instruct your old supervisor to contact you after hours. An exception to making such an offer to your old company would be if you've gone to work for a competitor. If this is the case, it's probably not even ethical for you to help your previous company and your new employer is almost sure to frown upon the idea of you helping your old employer.

Throughout the transition process at the company you're leaving, I suggest that you continue to maintain occasional contact with your new company, just to make sure everything continues to be "go". And, if you have any new questions that come up while you are waiting to start your new job, these occasional contacts will be good times to ask those questions of your future employer.

And finally, as you prepare to leave your old job for the new job, I'll remind you once again to "take the high road". Don't diss the company you're leaving, don't flaunt your new job to the co-workers you're leaving behind, and don't coast in your last days there. Continue to work hard, continue to display a positive and grateful attitude, and take the time to thank any people there who were helpful to you. Make the most of your remaining time there and create a smooth and pleasant transition from your old job to the exciting next chapter of your career.

How to Transform a Rejection into Something Positive.

So, you just got the dreaded "we've decided to go in a different direction" news. You're not going to get that job you had wanted so badly. What do you do now?

Well, first you should realize that life isn't all puppy dogs and balloons. We all get rejected at one time or another. One of the most difficult things about being a job applicant is that ultimately whether you get hired is beyond your control. I know people who swear that they did the best they could possibly do and it still wasn't enough to get the job. Some of those people even think they had the perfect interview; there was nothing they could have done better. Maybe they didn't have as much experience as other candidates, maybe they didn't have the skills that other candidates had. Either way, they didn't get the job.

I always encourage people who have been rejected in a job interview to maintain a positive attitude, to continue to focus on the process and not the results, and to look back and analyze the interview to see if there was anything they could have done better or could be doing better.

Here are some suggestions on things you can do after you've been rejected in an interview:

1) Ask for feedback. After you've been told that the company you interviewed with has decided to go in a different direction, ask for their feedback as to why you didn't get

Job Interview Preparation

the job. Ask this in a positive manner, not a defensive manner, and you might be surprised at how many hiring managers are forthcoming about why you didn't get the job. And, if you are working through a recruiter or headhunter to get a job, the same applies. Ask them to follow up with the employer to see where and why you came up short. You can use this information to evaluate the way you're interviewing. If you get rejected from multiple jobs for the same or similar reasons, you'll probably need to look at how you're interviewing or the positions you're interviewing for.

2) Analyze, identify, and adapt. It's important that you continue to analyze why you're not getting the jobs you're applying for. As mentioned above, if you can get feedback from the people you interviewed with, that will certainly help. But whether you get feedback from interviewers or not, you should constantly be analyzing your process and your performance in trying to get the jobs you want. Sure, it's possible that you might not be doing anything wrong at all, however you'll be selling yourself short if you don't at least step back and look for areas you could improve upon in your interviewing efforts.

3) Focus on things you can change. In some instances, you won't be able to make any changes based on the reason you didn't get the job. For example, I have a client from Illinois who recently applied for a sale position with a national firm. The sales position was responsible for two states, Louisiana and Texas. When my client found out that the

Job Interview Preparation

company he interviewed with had decided to go in a different direction, he asked the hiring manager if there was a reason they hadn't chosen him. The hiring manager noted that the candidate who was hired, had previous sales experience in those states and that's why they decided to go with him instead of my client. Well, this was something that was certainly beyond my client's control. He couldn't control where his territories were, and he had no knowledge of that going into the interview. Also, it was mere coincidence that the person who got the job had worked previously in those Louisiana and Texas. So, my client probably didn't do anything wrong in his interview process. Someone else was just lucky enough to have worked in those states before.

I'll giving you another story which illustrates how an applicant focused on the shortcomings he could change. A relative of mine is a baseball coach. I get the feeling that he's great at what he does, because I've read about his achievements on the internet. (Everything we read on the internet is true, right? Joke.) Well, for years, my relative had been a community college coach who has been interested to become a minor league batting coach and then eventually work his way up to being a major league batting coach. Over two years, he had interviews with four different minor league baseball teams and each time he came away empty. Frustrated, he finally decided to go back to the people he interviewed with and find out why they hadn't hired him and what the differences were between him and the persons they hired. The first two organizations he called were forthcoming enough to tell him that they were concerned with whether he would be able to work well with the Latin American players, as he did not speak Spanish. For those of you that don't know, there are a large percentage of Latin American players in the US minor and major baseball leagues and not all of them speak or understand English proficiently. So, armed with this information, my relative took it upon himself to take some accelerated Spanish classes. Sure enough, by the time the next season came around, he was very competent at speaking Spanish. He applied for a job as a minor league batting coach and he was hired. A couple lessons can be learned from his experience. First, he solicited feedback on why he'd been previously rejected. Second, he analyzed that information and determined that he probably wasn't winning those jobs because he didn't speak Spanish, even though that was never advertised as a requirement for the job. Third, he realized that he could change that deficiency and took some Spanish courses.

4) Promise to learn something from your rejection. It's no secret that we can learn a lot from our failures. And if we don't learn from our failures, we'll keep repeating them. If you've been rejected for a job, take it upon yourself to analyze what you could have done better and learn from it. Otherwise, all of the time and effort you spent preparing for that interview will surely go to waste. Try to take something valuable away from each rejection.

5) Refine your search. With the interview for the job you didn't get, was there anything you didn't like about the jobs or the companies you interviewed with? Rejection aside,

maybe you discovered some things about the job or the company that weren't as great as you thought they would be. If so, you might use this information to refine your search. As an example, if someone applies for an accounting management job and they realize from the interview that the job requires a lot more managing of people that it does accounting. And the person who applied for this job really isn't interested much in managing people. He would prefer more to be involved in just the accounting aspects of an accounting job. With that self-analysis, he can refine his future searches to accounting jobs that do not include management responsibilities.

6) Focus on the process, not the outcome. My clients will tell you that I harp on the idea that, in looking for a job, they need to focus on the process of going about getting a job and preparing and interviewing well instead of the outcome. Interviewing is a process and you won't be able to control the outcome of who is chosen for the job. However, if you can continue to fine tune the methods you are using to get and prepare for the interviews and continue to analyze and refine the way you're interviewing, you'll give yourself the best chance to manipulate the outcome. So, focus on the process and not the outcome.

Conclusion

So, there you have it. Now that you've read this book, you have the tools to go out and get the interviews you want. You also have some tips and techniques which should help you interview more successfully, be your best self, and land the job you really want.

We've discussed a variety of topics you can use in increase your chances of getting the job. You can get more interviews by using the tips I've given you to build a better resume. You can position yourself above other candidates by writing cover letters that will grab the reader and tell the interviewer why you are someone who is a formidable candidate who they have to interview.

We've discussed how to dress for an interview, how to overcome nervousness and anxiety. We've discussed the importance of doing your homework and researching the company you're interviewing with, so you can avoid the "So, what do you all do here?" question to start your interview. You should also have a better handle on how to navigate difficult questions in an interview and you now know what questions to ask during an interview. You know how to handle questions that catch you off-guard. With the right body language and an air of confidence, you'll be able to stand out and make a killer first impression. You now know what prospective employers want to hear and you know things they don't want to hear. And you know how to follow up after a job interview. If you're fortunate enough to become the leading candidate, you'll know how to negotiate to get the optimum salary. You'll also know what needs to happen after you accept an offer.

Bottom line, you now have the tools in your toolbox to score and ace interviews.

Job Interview Preparation

As I've mentioned before, the job interview process is a competition. You'll be competing against other candidates who have the same goal as you do—to get the job. If you're going to have a chance, you'll have to find a way to stand out from these other candidates. You're going to have to tweak and fine-tune your interview process. Although I've known people who have maintained that they had a perfect interview, but didn't get the job, I've always encouraged those people to continue to go back and analyze their process. Did they really do everything right? Isn't there something they could have improved upon?

Interviewing for a job can be a frustrating process, mostly because it includes some elements that are beyond your control. With the candidates who have felt that they've done everything right throughout the interview process, but still haven't landed the job, I tell them the same thing I'll tell you: In interviewing for jobs, it's important for you to focus on the process of getting the job, not the outcome. You can control what you do in your efforts to get the job, but you can't control whether you get the job. Unfortunately, that's beyond your control. So again, with those things in mind, focus on the process, not the outcome. If you can do that, I assure you that you'll have more success in getting interviews and you'll increase your chances of landing the job.

If you don't get a job, for whatever reason, don't hang your head. If you can learn from your past rejections, those rejections will ultimately help you improve your process. Yes, I have clients who tell me that they're tired of learning from their mistakes. That being said, I always remind them that searching for a new job is often a numbers game. It's a process, not an event. The more and the quicker you can fine-tune your process, the quicker you'll be able to land that new job.

You've now spent some of your valuable time in reading this book. I'm hoping that you'll now take the time to implement immediately some of the tips and techniques I've given you. With many self-help or "how to" books such as this one, readers make the mistake of not resolving to make changes immediately. They'll resolve to make changes someday, whenever they get around to it. Unfortunately, most of those people never get around to it. That's why I encourage you to make changes and change your process immediately. If you are willing to do that, you'll surely enhance your chances of getting the job you want. Although I can't guarantee that you'll get every job you apply for, I can say that if you use the tools I've provided, you'll be able to be your best self in trying to get interviews and you'll have a much better chance to succeed in the interviews you have.

So, let's get after it!

Wishing you more interviews and more interview success. Happy hunting!

www.ingramcontent.com/pod-product-compliance
Lightning Source LLC
Chambersburg PA
CBHW031128080526
44587CB00011B/1153